Brand Enigma

Decoding the Secrets of Your Brand

Duncan Bruce
and
David Harvey

WILEY

A John Wiley and Sons, Ltd., Publication

Other Wiley Editorial Offices

John Wiley & Sons Inc., 111 River Street, Hoboken, NJ 07030, USA

Jossey-Bass, 989 Market Street, San Francisco, CA 94103-1741, USA

Wiley-VCH Verlag GmbH, Boschstr. 12, D-69469 Weinheim, Germany

John Wiley & Sons Australia Ltd, 42 McDougall Street, Milton, Queensland 4064,
Australia

John Wiley & Sons (Asia) Pte Ltd, 2 Clementi Loop #02-01, Jin Xing Distripark,
Singapore 129809

John Wiley & Sons Canada Ltd, 6045 Freemont Blvd. Mississauga, Ontario, L5R 4J3
Canada

Wiley also publishes its books in a variety of electronic formats. Some content that
appears in print may not be available in electronic books.

Library of Congress Cataloging-in-Publication Data
Bruce, Duncan, 1951–
    Brand enigma : decoding the secrets of your brand / Duncan Bruce, David Harvey.
        p. cm.
    Includes bibliographical references and index.
    ISBN 978-0-470-77960-6 (cloth)
    1. Branding (Marketing)   2. Business names.   3. Corporate
image.   4. Organizational effectiveness.   5. Creative ability in business.
I. Harvey, David, 1945–   II. Title.
    HF5415.1255.B78 2008
    658.8'27 – dc22

                                                                              2008038615

British Library Cataloguing in Publication Data

A catalogue record for this book is available from the British Library

ISBN 978-0-470-77960-6

Typeset in SNP Best-set Typesetter Ltd., Hong Kong
Printed and bound in Great Britain by TJ International Ltd, Padstow, Cornwall, UK

CONTENTS

Contents

Contents

Contents

Contents

ACKNOWLEDGEMENTS

Many people have contributed, directly and indirectly, to the making of this book. Since the brand dream process continues to be work in progress, there are all those who have joined me at different stages of the journey and played a part in the adventure. Thanks are due to them, along with all those who generously agreed to share their experience of implementing brand dream and innovation programmes in their organisations that are included in the following chapters. Not only did they help to validate the brand dream model, but their feedback was invaluable in pointing to ways for refining the brand dream process further.

From these two groups, I should particularly like to mention Paul Stallard, Darrel Poulos, Giles Lenton, Heather Campbell, Marc Cox, Alan Sekers, Simon Williams, Debbie Taffler, Quinn Stainfield-Bruce, Richard Maryniak, Tom Morley, Sam Bond, Peter Moulin-Feroze, Natalie Bentley, Chris Priest, David Bott and Nick Shepherd.

Over the years a lot of other people, including clients, all my colleagues at the Brand Conspiracy and the Youth Conspiracy, not to mention friends, have helped more than they have realised in shaping my thinking about brands. There are really too many to mention by name, but I am sure they know who they are. To all of you, my heartfelt thanks.

Lastly, I should like to thank David Harvey, my co-conspirator on this project, who convinced me that there was something here that was too important to go unrecorded. The rest, as they say, is history.

Duncan Bruce

Executive Creative Director and Partner, The Brand Conspiracy

Prelude: Playing with Brands

Until I met and then later worked with Duncan, I had seen brands fulfilling a conventional marketing role as opposed to being the heartbeat of a business. Once I had become familiar with his philosophy and the way in which he worked with brands, I started to see things differently. Taking a brand dream perspective is like putting an enterprise on the psychiatrist's couch to find what really makes it tick. It provides an ordered way of testing the status and health of any brand and I began to play what-if? games based on the questions that the brand dream model poses. Here is one example.

One of my passions is music. Like all musicians, I am choosy about the instrument I play because I know that it makes a telling difference, psychologically as well as physically. If you are happy about the tone and sound quality you produce and feel comfortable with the way an instrument handles, then it adds immeasurably to your confidence as a player. After all, the instrument is an extension of you as a performer.

Ultimately, selecting an instrument comes down to how a particular horn feels and sounds when it is in your hands, and how you perform together as a unit. As a sax player, I have always taken a close-to-obsessive interest in everything to do with the main brands in the marketplace. I want to know about their origins, the people behind these companies, who else plays the same saxes, feedback from instrument repairers who strip them down and keep them running, what other musicians have to say about them. In short, I like to immerse myself in everything to do with their brand stories. Once I have homed in on a particular make, I file away all the facts and trivia that I have discovered about the maker, its traditions, reputation, strengths and weaknesses. Subliminally, all of this information influences the choice I make.

Over the years, I have owned several leading makes. But all that has really done is to confirm my first love. Despite a number of flirtations, I keep coming back to one leading brand.

For me and many others in the jazz community, Selmer is not just another marque. It defines the mysterious, edgy sound of jazz sax and has a legendary history that stretches way back to the earliest days of jazz. (Today, the brand is part of a much larger musical instrument-making empire of which saxophones represent only one division.)

Its saxes have their quirks and idiosyncrasies, but that is part of their unique character. When I play a Selmer,

I am conscious that I am not just holding a classic brand but tapping into a rich vein of musical history. Selmer's saxes have been used by many of the biggest names in jazz, including Paul Desmond, Wayne Shorter, John Coltrane, Michael Brecker, Sonny Rollins, Dexter Gordon, Stan Getz, Branford Marsalis, and the list extends to up-and-coming stars from the current generation. All contributed something of themselves to the genius of the brand.

Consciously or unconsciously, players who opt for a Selmer dream that some of that legendary magic will rub off on to them when they raise the mouthpiece to their lips, propel their breath through the instrument and make it their own. Secretly, you like to feel that you have joined one of the greatest jazz communities of all time, albeit as an associate rather than an honorary member.

More than that, I started to muse about the company as if I was the owner of its brand dream model. What should it do to continue to be part of the sax story? How should the company build on its traditions to sustain its reputation, ensure that it turns its passion for the Selmer sound into a bigger future that attracts new generations of customers, and what should it do to refresh the dream? For that matter, did it think about its brand in this kind of structured way and, if it were to do so, what difference would that make?

In many ways, the company shares a number of the universal challenges that haunt any brand builder today. Applying the brand dream model would start to clarify the opportunities and options ahead.

Looking at its brand balance sheet, the company has a number of exceptional assets to its name. On the credit side, it has an enviable reputation for creating fine instruments that has been built up over more than a century. It is well regarded in all branches of music, from classical to jazz and rock – in fact, in all the genres of music where saxes are played. It has benefited from word-of-mouth recommendations through the players' grapevine and the *de facto* endorsement of stars who command the admiration of both audiences and peer-group musicians. Furthermore, its status has been underwritten over the decades through recordings, interviews, articles, biographies and photographs of Selmer-playing stars. All of which adds up to a golden legacy that sets it aside from the competition.

But the past does not determine the future. There is no guarantee that it will continue to thrive on the basis of yesteryear's reputation. Selmer saxophones, like the renowned French vineyards, may have prided themselves on setting the world standard in their respective fields in the past. But in both markets, other makers from other countries have caught up and now offer products that are highly competitive and likely to continue to improve.

Also, Selmer is to some extent a victim of its own success. Such is the renown in which a number of its earlier marques are held that a thriving resale market has grown up and many of today's players seek out these vintage models. This has also created another source of competition. Much as Far Eastern motorbike makers have capitalised on the attraction of vintage Harley Davidson-style designs, so a number of newcomers have set out to emulate the qualities and sound of the legendary Selmer MkVI and other classic saxophones to capitalise on the market for that prized vintage sound.

This is a different market that continues to change. For Selmer saxes, the challenge is how to maximise the value of its brand in a market that is now fiercely contested by a number of other leading suppliers, as well as newcomers with competitive, professional-level models that give Selmer a run for its money. What can the market leader do to turn an illustrious past into a golden future?

In common with companies in other sectors, it has choices that revolve around brand extensions, enhancements and innovations. But beyond that, there are bigger questions about the Selmer brand today, the passion shared by those who work for the business and the dream that drives it onwards. Could it do more to amplify the messages about quality, tradition, the brand experience, mystique and its search for even greater performance values? This is one dream I would really like to be in on.

For Selmer, substitute any other name and the brand dream model can be used in just the same way to decode the key components of the brand. With super-abundant choice in the marketplace, a company's brand is its secret weapon, a differentiating asset that needs to be nutured and developed. I hope that this book will give anyone with a passion to succeed a new way of unlocking that secret and developing its full potential.

David Harvey

GETTING THE BEST FROM THIS BOOK

CHAPTER ONE

This is not a textbook on brand strategy or brand management, although it touches on these subjects. *Brand Enigma* takes as its theme the bigger role of brands in promoting organisational success. More specifically, it proposes an approach that can help to turn a brand into a business asset by making explicit the deeper, often hidden or forgotten drivers of success. Examples are taken mainly, but not exclusively, from the world of business.

Whether you are a small business, a school, a political party, a multinational, a municipal authority, an orchestra, a sports club or an entrepreneurial start-up, you have a brand. Your brand may be a global colossus. It may be niche. Or local and invisible to all but a handful of contacts. The brand may have been subject to detailed attention and lavish investment. It may have been neglected. Your brand may once have been great, but now in the doldrums. Your organisation may even be in denial that your brand plays any significant part in shaping your fortunes. Wherever you are on this spectrum, you can be certain that whether you like it or not, you have been branded – by everyone who knows you. They all have their own idea of what you stand for, which may be cause for delight or dismay, depending on their views.

Customers, suppliers, partners, employees or members of the community that deal with you all take away their ideas of what your organisation is about. Whether your brand is internationally recognised or local, well defined or confused and fuzzy, you will have made an impact, for better or worse, on all these groups. Like it or not, your brand is out there in the marketplace.

If your brand is strong, then it will have the virtues of commanding loyalty, inspiring referrals and working for you after hours when people meet, exchange views and experiences either face-to-face or, as is increasingly the case, over the Internet. If weak, your brand will be forgettable, eclipsed by discussion of your competitors. Your name may not even rate a mention in those offline discussions. Unless, of course, you are cursed with a pariah brand that is trashed at every opportunity by disaffected customers and contacts. Just as the Internet can amplify the good news, so gripe-and-grizzle websites have elevated one-to-one moans into global airings of dissatisfaction.

Most brand managers will not be surprised at any of this. But there are companies that have been slow to wake up to the reality of brand power. Not so long ago Ford sniffily maintained that it did not do brands. A *Business Week* article reported that Ford in 1999 had claimed: 'We aren't a consumer-goods company, and we don't have a brand.'[1] Of course the carmaker does, as others are all too well aware.

Ford's narrow definition did not prevent the auto company being rated the eighth most valuable brand in a 2001 global league table alongside other major non-consumer businesses including AT&T, GE, Nokia and Microsoft. The Ford misconception also belies the fact that brands have evolved to play a much wider role in the life of organisations over the generations. Brands may have come into their own as a consumer-goods phenomenon, but more and more of today's organisations, regardless of their sector or activity, recognise that they are a business asset for building value, creating loyalty, inspiring innovation and driving business growth.

League tables that rank brand worth also underline the point that there is serious money involved here. Rankings are a reminder of the contribution brands make to the intangible value of every business. Brands are part of the new wealth of companies – not just those operating in the consumer marketplace, but every kind of traded business. In the third millennium, the drivers of success are intellectual capital, knowledge, relationships, capabilities and all the other non-physical dimensions of the enterprise – including brands.

---

[1] 'The Best Global Brands', *Business Week*, pp. 44–55, 6 August 2001.

There is no denying Ford's brand value

It does not matter whether you sell subscriptions or soap, cars or computers, financial services or fridges, you can pin a dollar value on your organisation's brand over and above any plant, inventory or bricks and mortar assets. That is not all.

Brands play an equally important intangible role in the operational effectiveness of organisations. They may not have the buzz of a Gucci, Coca-Cola or Tommy Hilfiger, but any organisation's brand has the potential to raise performance to a new level when it is well defined and communicated effectively to the workforce and customers. Right from the start, the spirit of the brand can be crucial to sparking the energy and dynamism of an enterprise.

Brand redefined

By now it should be clear that the way in which the word brand is used in this book transcends the narrow sense of a logo, trademark or visible symbol of a company's identity. It has everything to do with the genius of the enterprise.

A brand, in our lexicon, is the sum total of everything that makes a product, service or organisation distinctive. A brand is the product of three components: its legacy and enduring traditions; its characteristic behaviour and culture; and the dream that sustains its continuing development.

Your brand is what you are all about, what makes your organisation competitive and gives it an edge – as well as where a considerable part of the business's value lies. It should be possible to summarise its essence in a handful of words. If you cannot pass the 15-word brand statement test, then you are going to struggle to get people to get what you are about, argues Tom Peters.

Even more important than being able to sum up the brand is the internalisation of what those words stand for. The brand dream needs to be real enough to everyone at every level of the organisation to inspire big decisions at the top as well as guide day-to-day processes and practices, dealings with customers, other stakeholders and so on. The spirit of the brand should permeate the whole organisation.

At one level, the brand dream acts as the compass for business strategy. It points to the best choices for selecting a new direction, diversification, innovation and all the good things that help an enterprise to expand and grow.

Branding, in this sense, is not something that can be applied cosmetically – a logo here, a new design there – to freshen up poorly performing products. Synthetic brands that are all surface and appearance do not pass the depth test or represent sustainable value. The brand is the product of everything that an organisation represents – its aspirations, history, expertise, knowledge and skills built up over time. It also reflects the organisation's corporate values and culture. Last, but by no means least, the brand embodies the bigger dream of what the enterprise sets out to achieve.

The secret of maximising the contribution and potential of every brand lies in gaining a deep understanding of its past and living traditions, its behaviour manifested in values and culture, as well as the inspiring dream that gives it forward momentum. Together, these generate the spirit of the brand. Some, or all, of these elements will need realignment over time. But without a reference point, the task of knowing how best to develop your brand's potential is tough or impossible to complete successfully.

Do not worry if you cannot instantly describe your brand in this structured, three-dimensional way. You are not alone. Even if one or more of these brand dimensions are in focus, it is unlikely that they are visible across the whole organisation. Few companies have achieved this degree of detailed insight into their brands, let alone a shared sense of the genius of the brand across all areas of the business. Outside the marketing department, many brands have never been defined and expressed coherently and consistently. Even when they have, it is in no more than general and vague terms. But codify your brand comprehensively, and all kinds of possibilities open up for your enterprise.

- First of all, there is a yardstick for making better-informed choices about new markets, innovation, brand extensions, major product launches and so on.
- Second, the brand can be used to prioritise performance goals that focus people's energy on activities and priorities that are aligned with brand goals.
- Third, your brand is integrated with your corporate culture, beliefs and values, so that the whole organisation knows what it means to live the brand.
- Fourth, marketing's job becomes clearer. Once the brand has been comprehensively described and internalised, brand promotion and development can be predicated on clear principles.
- Fifth, it smoothes the path to the creation of an employer brand with consistent values and objectives that creates a bridge between internal and external customers.

Establishing the genius of the brand is the first step to raising your performance to a higher competitive league. A well-conceived, properly integrated brand represents an asset that should be measurable in terms that make sense to everyone from the finance director to the workforce and shareholders.

How dreams and visions produce hard results

Companies tend to choose their words carefully when they talk in public about the driving force behind their business. Strategy, goals, mission statements and even visions are part of the acceptable language for describing corporate results in investor relations and annual reports. But many big company successes owe their success to something that is much more powerful and elusive. Behind virtually every great brand there is an inspiring dream.

Many of the most successful businesses got off the ground because the founder dreamed of possibilities that were outrageously ambitious, punch-the-air inspiring, or in contravention of the received wisdom of the time. Business originals like Apple's Steve Jobs, the late Anita Roddick – founder of Body Shop – and Nike's Phil Knight show that passionate belief in what others may consider to be impossible or absurd, coupled with a gift for leadership, can put the naysayers in their place. They are members of a dynasty of big dreamers who show that shooting for the stars can pay off. Dreamers are often rule-breakers.

At the dawn of mass motoring in 1907, Henry Ford set his sights on a goal that was typically bold when he announced his plan to:

'... build a motor car for the great multitude. It will be large enough for the family, but small enough for the individual to run and care for ... so low in price that no man making a good salary will be unable to own one.'[2]

---

[2] *The Meaning of Technology*, edited by Montserrat, Ginés Edicions UPC, 2003, p. 60.

Nice idea. But how? No one knew how this could be done at that time. In the teeth of dismissive scepticism, he pioneered the production line and confounded his doubters. Others have also built extraordinary success on the back of their dreams. Back in the 1890s City Bank, a tiny regional bank with only a handful of staff, set itself the audacious target of becoming 'a great national bank'. It might have looked hopelessly optimistic then. Today, in its current incarnation as Citicorp, the bank has wildly overachieved its national aspirations to become one of the world's largest companies.

Or like Dave Packard – co-founder of Hewlett Packard, the electronics to computing company – whose lofty vision was to create a model business that would be a benchmark for breakthrough innovation, world-class products and progressive people practices. 'Our main task,' he said, 'is to design, develop, and manufacture the finest electronic equipment for the advancement of science and the welfare of humanity.'[3]

But what if you succeed in realising your dream only for others to start to muscle in on the game and overhaul you? Which was exactly what happened to Ford after it opened the way to mass-production car making and General Motors

---

[3] Quoted from HP archives in *Built to Last*, James C. Collins & Jerry I. Porras, Century, 1996, p. 207.

picked up the lead. There is no guarantee that every dream, however compelling, will translate into a great business. Even some brands that take off promisingly at first can veer off course.

When dreams lose their magic

Realising and sustaining brand success is hard work, and there are all sorts of reasons why a great dream can lose its inspirational magic or turn into a nightmare.

There are plenty of companies that have taken a wrong turning, never managed to find their way back to a profitable path, and crashed and burned. There are cases where companies have confronted potential disaster but rebounded strongly: Harley Davidson and IBM both had their mid-life crises but rebuilt their businesses and rekindled the flame of success. Their stories can be read from a number of perspectives: business strategy, competitive manoeuvres, market trends, leadership and organisational capability. But their stories are also traceable as the history of their brands.

Take Starbucks, a brand that pioneered the coffee experience through its 'third place' outlets, created as an in-between work and social environment for meeting over a cup of coffee. Yet after 20 years of impressive growth since its launch in 1987, the Starbucks brand started to lose momentum. Despite generating $12bn from its 15,000 outlets scattered around the globe, Starbucks was no longer the roaring success it had been a few years ago when the talk had been of more than doubling the number of outlets in the near future.

Having moved upstairs a few years ago to become chairman, Howard Schultz returned as CEO to inject new life into what had become an underperforming brand. The coffee store pioneer had seen competitors pile into the marketplace, some of which went head-to-head with the company while others, including McDonald's and Dunkin' Donuts, came in from their own established base with a direct appeal to coffee drinkers. But it was not just competition that started to blunt the coffee chain's advantage. Schultz saw that the brand itself had become lacklustre and had begun to neglect what had made it successful.

'We somehow evolved from a culture of entrepreneurship, creativity and innovation to a culture of, in a way, mediocrity and bureaucracy,' said Schultz. 'We have somehow lost our edge.'

The proliferation of ever-more-exotic flavoured coffees had replaced inspirational innovation, while the once-coffee-rich aroma that had wafted out of its doors was eclipsed by the smell of other foodstuffs. With growth had come the downsides of bloated organisational structure and management overload.

Starbucks found its pioneering position under siege

Its attempts at merchandising other products such as CDs had met with indifferent success. On his return as CEO, Schultz reviewed the traditions that had made Starbucks great as part of his review of the options for the company's revival and future development. The challenge for Starbucks was to rediscover the spirit of its brand, build on the strengths of the past and conjure a new dream for the next phase of growth.

Discover the genius behind your brand

All these examples illustrate the importance of understanding the genius of your brand. What made a brand special in the first place may no longer be relevant after changes in the marketplace have created new conditions for success and ignited different customer demands. Deconstructing and reassembling the core elements of the brand can enable you to discover what needs to be updated, revised or reinvigorated. The process may also reveal an untapped opportunity, throw light on the reasons why things went wrong, or show how to rekindle the spirit of the brand. Even companies that think they know their brands well are surprised at the way in which that very familiarity can blind them to important factors and issues. Just as critical, using the spirit of the brand as the touchstone for decisions about diversification could steer you away from poor choices, such as diversification into product lines that add no value or dissipate energy and resources.

The act of retracing the brand story and reliving its ups and downs can reveal forgotten clues that explain what helped the brand to soar or falter in the marketplace. Key events may not necessarily have occurred at the birth of the company, but later in its history. 3M only discovered a profitable direction after a near-disastrous start in mining gave way to the launch of a range of abrasives. Whatever the inspirational driving force for success, it will have generated traditions and values that connect the past with the present. Bringing the story up to date means looking at the current behaviour of the brand – not just its manifestation in marketing terms, but in the way it influences the behaviour of the company, how it is seen by those who work in the organisation and how it is regarded in the marketplace. The process needs to be honest and rigorous, flushing out the negative as well as the positive attributes of the brand.

Determination to uncover the folklore and the facts should be part of your agenda. The manner in which you set about decoding your brand is just as important. What you will find in the following chapters is a radically different, fresh approach that may appear unorthodox, but is rooted in ideas that have stood the test of time and are now being validated by leading-edge research in psychology, perception and cognition.

The brand dream process and the accompanying brand dream model are a pragmatic response to the frustrations that companies experience in relating brand development to corporate strategy and the bigger picture. It enables people to search for answers through their intuition and look for inspiration and insights that come from their experience and personal knowledge. It is an approach that redresses the balance and is complementary with, not a substitute for, analysis and discussion.

It is also a process that should help companies to rebalance their thinking. The development of specialist marketing and brand functions can be part of the problem. When companies concentrate responsibility in these departments, the result can be a siloed organisation where new product development and other sections of the business become detached from brand building and maintenance. The shared responsibility for the brand is lost.

It is easy to see how the straight line between an inspirational dream and strategy becomes broken over time. Whether it is because the founding entrepreneur is no longer at the helm, or the dream has been rendered obsolete because the mountain has already been climbed, or smarter competitors have stolen the initiative, the challenge is to revitalise or renew the dream so that the organisation can be re-energised for a new phase of growth.

Built to Last authors Collins and Porras dug into the stories behind enduring brands and came up with a dramatic finding. It is only when a visionary capability is embedded in the organisation that businesses are able to constantly renew the goal that drives them forward. It is rarely good enough to have one vision, however compelling, in the history of a business. You need to be a serial dreamer to sustain success. Great dreams fulfilled become yesterday's stories. Or they are marginalised by others' bigger, better dreams. Even then, visions of possibilities are no more than that unless they are translated into strategies and plans that generate hard results.

That has to be a given, but the ability to implement is by no means all there is to it. Dreams need to be authentic. It has been fashionable to chide companies for lacking a clear vision for directing their business. Which might have been good news for consultants all too happy to help visionless companies fashion chic statements that looked and sounded like the real thing, but were all surface and no substance. Having a vision statement does not mean that you have passed the test, unless the words stand for something real and meaning-ful. It needs to be visible in the culture of the company and integrated everywhere from plans and goals to peo-ple's behaviour and values. Going into megaphone mode with italics and exclamation mark, Collins and Porras want people to know that the piece of paper is not enough.

'Just because a company has a "vision statement" (or some-thing like it) in no way guarantees that it will become a visionary company!' [4]

What passes the drop test for them is the organisation that 'creates a total environment that envelops employees, bom-barding them with a set of signals so consistent and mutu-ally reinforcing that it's virtually impossible to misunderstand the company's ideology and ambitions.'[5]

Saturating the company with an understanding of what the brand is about, its objectives and aspirations is one way of achieving that goal. The remainder of *Brand Enigma* is dedicated to showing how taking a step sideways can enable you to see your brand in a new light and develop its potential for the whole business.

- Chapter One
  Getting the best from this book

If you have got this far, then you should know that this present chapter sets the scene for the book and describes the territory that is covered, the terms of reference and the defini-tion of brand that is used throughout the following chapters.

---

[4] *Built to Last,* James C. Collins & Jerry I. Porras, Century, 1996, p. 201.
[5] Ibid, p. 202.

- Chapter Two

  Nightmares and dreams: the new world of brands

This puts brands into the bigger context of business. It looks at the drivers of change and growth and their implications for brands. In addition, it identifies some of the risks and opportunities that companies face as a result of the major trends in globalisation of markets, the continuing rise of the Internet and the shift in power from marketers to consumers. Chapter Two also traces the history of brands and reviews the various roles that they can play from establishing owner-ship and differentiation in the marketplace through to their role in creating a customer experience and customer loyalty. The chapter concludes with a self-assessment test to highlight brand issues in your organisation.

- Chapter Three

  Enduring myths, new challenges and realities

Effective development of brands is only going to take place once companies accept that there is some housekeeping to be done before moving on to the exciting stuff.

— Myth One: Brands are just about differentiation in the marketplace.
— Myth Two: What you see is all you get.
— Myth Three: Brands only concern the marketing department.

— Myth Four: Customers are the only brand consumers that count.
— Myth Five: External research will tell you all you need to know about your brand.
— Myth Six: You can bury the bad news.
— Myth Seven: With the internationalisation of markets, it is easy for brands to act globally.

Next, the chapter outlines four challenges that are key to understanding the changing role of brands.

— Challenge One: Do you confuse new product development and innovation with brand extension?
— Challenge Two: Do you think that you are the real owner of your brand?
— Challenge Three: Is your brand development two paces behind the competition?
— Challenge Four: Do you still believe you have a unique selling point?

This leads on to a discussion of some of the cardinal rules for developing brands.

— Rule One: Brands are too important to be left to the brand manager.
— Rule Two: Brands need to be reviewed and renewed.
— Rule Three: The leader is the brand.

— Rule Four: Brand reputation may not be easily quan-
tifiable, but it is a major asset.
— Rule Five: A brand should be one of the most important drivers of performance at every level of the
business.
— Rule Six: Get in touch with the spirit of the brand
to discover its transformational power.

• Chapter Four
How the brand dream process took shape

This explains how the process for decoding the secrets of
brands was developed and refined. Outlining the brand
issues is one thing. Finding a way for companies to move
from understanding the challenges to coming up with creative solutions involved following a different path. What they
needed was a way of generating actionable insights –
standard conventional methods of brand development were
generating uninspiring and flat results for people. Convinced
that the answers had to lie in methods and techniques based
on radically different approaches, our search for a better way
led to explorations of both new and old thinking. The resulting brand dream process is based on a range of ideas drawn
from psychology, Eastern, Native American traditions and the
arts. The common denominator underlying all phases of the
process is that they are experiential in nature. They involve
people at an intuitive level and lead to a shared consensus

of what are the most important features of the brand. Six principles underpin the brand dream process.

— Principle One: If you stay on the surface you will never understand what lies underneath.
— Principle Two: Location, location, location – never underestimate the magical power of place to energise or demotivate the creative process.
— Principle Three: Use all your faculties, not just your intellect, to see things in new ways.
— Principle Four: Conventional methods produce conventional results. Trust your intuition to lead you where you need to go.
— Principle Five: If you are not enjoying yourself and thinking intuitively, then you are not going to be creative.
— Principle Six: Once you change the way you feel about the whole brand experience, you can change the way the brand behaves.

• Chapter Five
  Fitting the pieces together: the brand dream model

The brand dream model is deceptively simple. It is built around three aspects of the brand: its living traditions; the way the brand behaves; and the dream, the sustaining vision of the enterprise. Another way of seeing the three circles of the model is in temporal terms: traditions (past); behaviour (present); and the dream (future). The symbolism of the model shows that the genius of the brand is the summation of its three component parts. The few words that end up in each circle may look sparse but they are heavy with meaning and significance for those who fashioned them. These terse statements represent the end point of a process that involves the kinds of experiential activities described in more detail in the preceding chapter. Both the process and the model are totally interdependent. And the way that the model is constructed is as important as the resulting model itself.

- Chapter Six
  Taking the brand dream medicine

Sponsors who between them have been responsible for six brand dream projects talk about their experience, why they decided to follow this programme and what it generated in terms of outputs and results. They also talk about the issues for them personally in adopting what one called a 'high-risk, high-return' approach. The individual accounts trace the different goals and circumstances for these organisations. Overwhelmingly, the project sponsors found that they achieved results that would have been impossible using other means. Other important bonuses included the development of a consensus around the brand's values and key attributes.

- Chapter Seven
  Deconstructing brands: a new way of sussing out the competition

While the primary purpose of the brand dream process and model is to give you a new way of seeing your own brand and developing its potential, the model can also be applied to deconstruct other brands. In the same way that it can be used to unearth clues about the strengths and weaknesses of your own brand, it can be applied as a diagnostic tool to understand other organisations. This can be useful whether the need is simply to gain a better understanding of competitors or to size up a prospective partner or acquisition target. So although the real power of the brand dream model comes from applying it from the inside of an organisation, using the framework to think your way into the brand of a competitor in a structured way can yield some surprising insights. To illustrate its use in this way, we have generated brand dream models for a range of organisations, not just businesses but charities and state-run corporations: BBC, Google, Marks & Spencer, Nike, Oxfam, Ryanair, Virgin.

- Chapter Eight
  Engaging staff in the employer brand

The process is not only concerned with the outward-facing aspect of your brand. Enabling the workforce to get in touch with the spirit of the brand can help to re-energise the enterprise and bring a renewed sense of drive and purpose to everything it does. In the era when no chairman's report is complete without the claim that 'People are our greatest asset', the need to build engagement, commitment and loyalty inside the organisation has become a universal priority. Companies that work hard at making their employer brand as strong as their customer brand have a real advantage over those who merely trot out the people-asset mantra.

Business leaders who are natural enthusiasts understand instinctively how to convey the spirit of the brand as much through their actions as in what they say. The challenge for organisations that have moved beyond the days when the founder was in charge is how to sustain that brand advocacy and energy in-house. With success comes growth, staff turnover, multiple locations, larger-scale operations and mixed messages. Keeping people focused on the dream is no longer so simple. The brand dream process offers companies a practical way of developing a shared experience of the spirit of the brand.

- Chapter Nine
  A web of threats and opportunities

The Internet has massive implications for brands. Along with the ever-growing importance as a sales channel, the web has changed the rules of engagement with an inexorable shift in power from companies to customers. No longer is it possible for companies to dictate the communications agenda. The democratisation of the web has resulted in radical changes in the way in which consumers gather information about brands and can also influence the way in which they are perceived. But there are also opportunities for brand building, if companies are ready to play by the rules.

- Chapter Ten
  An inspirational approach to innovation

Companies are obsessed with innovation, but few have found the secret of developing the processes and practices that deliver bottom-line results. Many companies are stuck with mechanistic and unproductive innovation methods. But using similar experiential techniques and approaches to those that underpin the brand dream process, companies can create conditions that stimulate serendipity, inspired hunches, even sheer brilliance.

NIGHTMARES AND DREAMS: THE NEW WORLD OF BRANDS

CHAPTER 2

'Products are built in factories, brands are built in the mind.'

David Ogilvy

The early days of the third millennium will go down in history for many reasons, good and bad, inspiring and depressing. Digital technology, scientific advances on every front from medicine to nanotechnology, global warming and the rise in eco-consciousness, the Internet, the growing gulf between rich and poor nations, oil wars and acts of genocide, the power of multinational business and the growing awareness of the interconnectedness of everything from economies to weather systems. This is the era of the iPhone, catastrophe theory, Google, sub-prime mortgages, the carbon footprint, genetic medicine, cheap air travel, international terrorism, organic food, reality TV, instant celebrity. It has also been a stern test of the way in which companies run all aspects of their business, from people and innovation to their environmental and social policies. In this period of churning change, brands have also entered a new roller-coaster era.

As the commercial world revved up to cruising speed, brands played an increasingly important part in sustaining and leading business growth. A glance back over the recent past reveals that while some brands have burnt brightly but briefly, others have weathered the good and bad times to demonstrate a remarkable resilience in the face of changing tastes, fads and trends. Big names like Coca-Cola and Disney have managed to discover the secret of long life. But even these icons of brand success are eclipsed in terms of longevity by less well-known names like Lyle's 121-year-old Golden Syrup, which wins the *Guinness Book of Record's* accolade for the world's most venerable brand. But record-breakers are by definition the exception. Life for most brands and businesses has become increasingly precarious. There is no certainty that what worked yesterday will guarantee success tomorrow. Look at the Fortune 500. Today's list contains only a handful of companies that figured in the premier league 40 years ago.

To survive and prosper, companies have to learn to change and constantly reinvent themselves. Whether their brands turn into prisons that keep them locked in the past, or are transformed into a source of inspiration for future evolution and growth all depends on an ability to ask the right questions and find illuminating answers.

Those who have got it right know that powerful brands are capable of generating extraordinary results. They can command lifetime loyalty, and inspire boundless enthusiasm that spills over into spontaneous recommendations that are worth their weight in advertising schedules. For power brands such as Apple, Nike, Starbucks and Harley Davidson, the buzz seems to come naturally. That, of course, is just the way it may appear. The energy that goes into effortless performance is considerable. Even for the top performers, it is never as simple as that. At some time or another every company, including several of these major brands, runs into difficulties that severely test their confidence in their brand strengths as well as their ability to turn that confidence into fresh business opportunities.

Strong brands have a number of characteristics: they are instantly recognisable, they have a well-defined position in the marketplace, they are consistent, their reputation is clear-cut, customers identify closely with their values – or know to steer well clear of them. However, just becoming well known and highly visible does not guarantee brand success.

When *Marketing* magazine and the communications consultancy Joshua ran their 2006 most-loved and most-hated brand survey they came up with some revealing findings. Topping the most-loved category was Google. Most-hated was Pot Noodle, which had the distinction of emulating its previous year's performance, but with even more votes. The distance between fame and notoriety can be small.

Harley Davidson found the road back to renewed growth

Welcome to the era of warp-speed change

If businesses operate in a world of radical discontinuity and confusion, it is also one that generates extraordinary new opportunities. From a brand perspective, the twenty-first century throws down challenges of a kind and intensity for which there are no rulebooks and reliable maps. Confidence about what brands stand for – and how they operate – has never been more central to success.

On the negative side of the sheet, there's enough to turn a nail-biter into a full-blown neurotic. A quick scan of the press and media coverage confirms that what Peter Drucker – the sage of management practice – predicted a couple of decades ago in his book *The Age of Discontinuity* is here with a vengeance.

With competition coming from every which way, consumer expectations shifting with often unpredictable consequences, internationalisation – and instant communications – shrinking the world to a global village and new technologies under-mining established businesses, there's little time to think or react. The unceasing blast of disruptive events is enough to test the nerves of the most resilient. It is tempting to think that the best that can be done is just to hang on to the roller-coaster until it slows. Only the pace isn't going to slacken. We will have to learn to live with the white-knuckle syndrome.

With so much uncertainty, unpredictability and chaos brewing in the marketplace right now, it is little wonder that there is a strong temptation to focus on today and resist thinking about what might be round the corner. But fire-fighting today's problems never has been a strategy. It calls for a deal of courage and vision, but taking a view of the next wave of changes and what they could mean for business is one way to retain some control of the future. Scanning the near horizon shows that there's plenty to think about. These are just some of the mega-forces that ensure the ride is – depending on your perspective – either extremely scary or exhilarating.

- Disruptive technologies. The kind that can whip your market away from you while you watch in disbelief. What happened to the wind-up watch industry could be about to happen to print-based information suppliers as the worldwide web takes over, or to telcos as Internet-based communications take off.
- Pendulum swings in social and ethical values can bury old industries and create new ones. The rise of fair trade and organics is driven by deeply felt beliefs and convictions. Thus, yesterday's favourite can become tomorrow's pariah – furs, once the emblem of elegance, became a symbol of exploitation and unacceptable consumerism.
- Competition. Lots more of it, from left field as well as existing competitors.

- Global warming. The knock-on effect from this shift in the earth's climate is unpredictable and potentially overwhelming, and already being felt.
- Chain-reaction changes. Whether triggered by new technologies, competition or other drivers, each fresh upheaval ripples through the marketplace to set off after-shocks that precipitate further changes and new regulations. It simply never stops.

It is not a business environment for the weak-willed or faint-hearted. But as IBM rather tritely lectured its staff, there are no problems, only opportunities. Microsoft, Apple and other banner-carriers for the new technological age would agree.

While every industry has its own set of local factors to contend with, several of the drivers of change are universal and unavoidable in their effect. None more so than the Internet, which has risen from nowhere to create a whole new dimension for trading for business and consumers, plus new channels for business and personal communication and information-sharing.

By 2008, there were billions of web pages and growing. No one knows for sure how many sites are out there, but a loosely defined Google search can turn up millions of citations: brands generated 264 million references, for example.

Not bad for an infant phenomenon that had hardly climbed out of the cradle fifteen years ago. Notwithstanding its youth, the web has created a whole new class of mega brands.

Changing everything at Internet speed

In little more than a decade, the Internet has grown into a powerhouse of innovation. It is the home of some of the world's best-known and dynamic brands. Names that were not even heard of a decade or so ago are now familiar around the world.

- Google, the world's favourite search engine, has grown at record speed and now straddles the globe from America to China.
- eBay, the online auction site, has created an international marketplace for everything and anything from Far East electronics and vintage cars to attic-hoarded toy cars and household junk.
- Amazon, the books-to-everything online store, challenged retailing orthodoxy by setting up shop in cyber space and established itself as the world's most widely recognised web retailer.
- MySpace, Facebook and Twitter are some of the new breed of social networking forums that have brought personal communications to a completely new level of sophistication.

In the pre-web world, it took companies like GE, Exxon, Coca-Cola and Disney generations to build their empires and brands. Internet years are equivalent to decades in the industrial era, enabling today's web goliaths to achieve establishment status in a fraction of the time.

Nor is it only the newcomers who are carving out fortunes. Some of those grounded in the world of bricks-and-mortar business have also got their minds round the web's potential and are moving fast. Tesco, the supermarket giant, claims to be the world's largest online grocery store.

Opportunities for creating web-based businesses that would simply have been impossible pre-Internet are on the positive side of the change account. The whole Web 2.0 phenomenon poses questions that put many sectors on the spot. Some, like retailing, are finding that these are interesting times. It is not simply that e-commerce is siphoning spend from the high street. The web has been instrumental in redefining the rules of engagement, particularly the supplier–customer relationship and, by extension, brand building.

Globalisation, fair trade and ethical business

It has been creeping up on the world for the past few decades, but the consequences of the shift in economic power are written on packaging in every retail outlet. As the Far East has taken on the role of the industrial powerhouse of the world, buyers of anything from trainers to tee-shirts, cars to cosmetics, saucepans to saxophones will find that the majority of these and other goods are made in China and its neighbouring countries. Long gone are the days when Western brands meant Western manufacturing. It is the same with food. Fresh fruit and vegetables are as likely to be flown in from Peru, Kenya or New Zealand as delivered from local sources.

At the same time, nations and consumer groups have started to ask questions about the behind-the-scenes facts, including evidence of socially responsible corporate behaviour, the conditions under which products are produced and the implications for the environment. Many of the world's poorest producers have become more vocal in lobbying for a fairer share of this new economic bounty. Consumer groups have similarly drawn attention to the working conditions and environmental impact involved in sourcing and transporting these products half way round the world. The concept of fair trade has entered the vocabulary of retailers and major brands.

An unstoppable chain reaction

Nothing occurs in isolation. What may seem to be a well-defined set of issues quickly spills over into other areas of concern. Globalisation raises questions about carbon footprint and the comparative merits of local versus overseas production. Then there are the competing cases for the trade-off between air freighting beans from Kenya and supporting family incomes in these poorer economies and the deficit in the carbon burning account. This in turn influences consumer attitudes and behaviour and introduces another factor in buying decisions.

Brands in the dock

In this heady atmosphere, it is no wonder that the rules of engagement have changed substantially and the ways in which brands behave come under critical scrutiny. At different times they have been put in the dock for variously operating as enemies of the consumer. Ralph Nader – the American consumer champion – first waged war in the 1970s on companies that put corporate profits before consumer safety, especially in the automobile market. More recently, he has challenged their commitment to planet-friendly technologies. With the rise of super brands, more companies have come under fire for growing their power by exploiting producers of raw materials and products and hoodwinking the consumer in the process.

One of the most recent high-profile inquisitions into brand exploitation of product suppliers and consumers was carried out by Naomi Klein, whose book *No Logo*[6] argued the case

---

[6] *No Logo*, Naomi Klein, Flamingo, 2000.

that major brands were unscrupulously fleecing an unsuspecting public and exploiting low-wage producers. Big brands are bad, was the message.

While brand power can be abused, it is neither inevitable nor universally the case. There is nothing intrinsically good or bad about the practice of branding. Brands can lie and deceive. They can also tell the truth. At different times and in different hands, brands have and continue to play a number of constructive roles that work to the advantage of supplier and consumer.

In the early days of the growth of commerce and consumerism, brands became a valuable means of distinguishing between reliable and unreliable goods. In the case of food, packaged goods from a branded source provided one way in which consumers could be reassured that what they were buying was safe and wholesome, compared with unbranded alternatives. That purpose continues up to the present day. People are used to relying on brand reputation to sift the good from the bad. Rankings of brand price/performance for everything from utilities to financial services, cars to washing machines have become a staple of consumer decision-making. It is not only in the marketplace that brands have become a more significant factor. Their significance extends to the corporate balance sheet and is a factor in mergers, flotations and other transactions where value has to be assessed.

Brands are now recognised as business assets in their own right, with a value that transcends the badging of services and products. They are regarded as a unique transferable asset, with an earnings potential that is based on their historic record, market trends and performance potential. The need to account for brand value is part of the drive to account for the fact that an ever-higher proportion of corporate worth is ascribable to intangible assets. It is not the only way in which the brand landscape has changed.

The democratisation of power and influence

Gone are the days when companies called the shots, could build their brands and promote them imperiously in the marketplace. The web has given customers far more influence than many suppliers may either realise or welcome. For better or worse, customers share their views through public forums, gossip openly and even set up campaigning websites that can support or dent corporate reputations and brands whether companies like it or not. Despite their lack of large budgets or sophisticated marketing teams, individuals can have a disproportionate influence on how companies and products are perceived through the web. This is the democratisation of information and communications in action.

This shift in the balance of power goes further, deeper and has moved faster than anyone would have guessed a few years ago. Listen to people like bestselling author, entrepreneur, agent of change and former Yahoo marketing chief Seth Godin, and he will tell you that the web has blown away the whole house of cards that represented traditional marketing. The rise of viral and permission marketing has given customers an unprecedented influence on brand standing. Once upon a time, word-of-mouth was a one-to-one phenomenon. Today, the web amplifies a whisper of complaint or praise into a global declaration. Brand building is no longer one-way traffic.

The problem is that much corporate thinking is stuck in an era when companies had a virtual monopoly on communications. Marketing departments spoke and consumers listened. This is no longer tenable in an era of growing customer power. So where does this leave brands?

Paradoxically, at the same time it leaves them both more vulnerable and potentially more powerful. They can become victims of changed circumstances, or benefit by becoming a master of the new rules of business. One thing is certain, though. Brand philosophy and brand strategy need to be reinvented to ensure that they represent assets, not liabilities. Aside from anything else, now that brands are coming under greater scrutiny than ever before from investors, consumers and lobby groups, they need to be ready to pass closer examination for consistency, trustworthiness and transparency. Credibility can no longer be taken for granted.

There is another twist in the brand saga that illustrates the tenuous hold that companies have on the integrity of their brands. Several companies have woken up with a shock to realise that their brands may have been of their own making, but like unruly teenagers, they can start behaving in ways that can cause alarm.

Brands that run riot

Most companies do their best to control their brands, but they are not always successful. Legal ownership of a brand is only part of the story. Trademarks, logos and copyrighted promotional and advertising material can prove weak defences once consumers start to impose their own counter-culture spin on brand values and standards. When brands start to keep strange company, all sorts of bizarre things can happen.

A number of examples show what happens when a brand is hijacked by groups who represent the polar opposite of the target market. Burberry knows how that feels. The brand had become the badge of the smart, along with their associated lifestyle and set of values, but then was adopted by Chavs – a downmarket UK youth movement with a taste for aping and sending up upmarket fashion in a way that had the company burying its corporate head in its hands.

When photos of a former TV soap-star – Danniella West-brook – and her baby, both topped out in trademark Burberry check, appeared in the tabloids, the once classy icon took a dive that it had never anticipated nor planned. Like an unstoppable virus, this fashion satire spread nation-wide as UK market stalls started shifting imitation Burberry gear by the ton as Chavs everywhere donned their new uniform. Burberry became the butt of sniggering fun in the press. And it hurt. Both the brand and the company's UK fortunes were undermined in the wake of this rampant savaging.

Things went from bad to worse. Burberry's image suffered further ignominy when the distinctive checked baseball caps, intended to adorn the heads of the smart set, were jammed gleefully on top of football hooligans' shaven heads. In a travesty of the company's cultivated image, the brand became involuntarily associated with crude, anti-social skinhead loutishness.

Burberry's response: removal of the distinctive checked base-ball caps from sale and the playing down of the distinctive pattern that had adorned a fifth of all its products in the early 2000s. Sales of these products fell to 5% by 2004. Burberry also launched an assault on the fakes which had made it all too easy for the wrong types to parody the brand. Nonethe-less, the brand survived this episode and overcame the set-backs with renewed growth.

Nor was Burberry the first designer label to be dragged from middle-class respectability into ignominious company. Back in the 1980s some Liverpool football supporters adopted Fred Perry jumpers, while in the USA Tommy Hilfiger became the favoured gear of warring rappers. This, says Dr Peter Marsh – co-director of the Social Issues Research Centre in Oxford – is social irony in action.

'People are trying to identify who they are and it's very ironic that they are choosing the garb of the upper middle class and turning it right around. What we are seeing is a lovely sign of irony. Early skinheads adopted the signs of the working class with braces and jeans. Mods and Rockers each had their own images, and Burberry's clothes are undergoing the same experience, they have been borrowed by groups.'[7]

But was Burberry impotent to stop this sort of trashing of its brand? Or did the company contribute to its own problems?

Raymond Boyle, a lecturer at Stirling University and a popular culture specialist, says:

'Burberry is a brand established for the elite and the affluent, which has rapidly expanded. At some point someone in the

---

[7] *Scotsman*, 4th December 2003.

marketing department said: "If we can bring it slightly down-market, we can increase the sales." But the result is that it gets picked up by popular culture and swept away. It's worn by celebs, over-worn by neds, then there is a fashion back-lash against it.'[8]

Its experience is not unique. Going mass-market can do more harm than good to a premium brand. Back in the 1980s, Calvin Klein was at its designer peak and allure. Thanks to the cheaper CK diffusion line, everyone was able to sport the label and its cachet was eroded. Similarly, Ralph Lauren – a name associated for years with top-quality cloth-ing – undermined its brand when its Polo range made the name synonymous with mass-merchandise.

Every company wants to make the most of its brands. It is just that some options have a large red danger flag flying over them.

However, this kind of unintended adoption can play to a brand's advantage. Since its launch in 1903, Harley Davidson has produced big bikes for serious bikers. There was nothing compromising about the evolution of the marque over the generations, which has weathered economic, competitive and consumer ups and downs. Harleys were meant for people who liked chunky, powerful machines that looked

---

[8] *Scotsman*, 4th December 2003.

macho and sounded unapologetically throaty. Only in one of those twists of fortune, Harleys became cool and in the process moved up a class or two. Wall Street bankers, top-notch lawyers and high-flying accountants developed a taste for what might have been the preferred bikes of the US police, but owed rather more of their mystique to their association with Hells Angels and tearaways. Their fame can also be traced to a long list of co-starring roles in hundreds of films, from *The Wild One*, featuring Marlon Brando as the Harley-riding hard man with a conscience, *Easy Rider*, with the road warriors Peter Fonda and Dennis Hopper, to *Terminator*, featuring Arnold Schwarzenegger who, as California governor, continued to gun his own Harley Davidson in his spare time.

Today, Harley Owners Group claims one million members and has chapters of bikers around the world made up of enthusiasts who are as likely to be sedate accountants or retired dreamers out for a weekend spin as youthful wild things. According to its own stats, the median age of Harley owners is pushing 50 with spending power in the mid-$80,000 bracket. And both demographics are on an upward curve.[9]

Its rebirth as a middle-class, middle-age favourite has helped the brand to emerge from a shaky period a few generations

---

[9] http://www.harley-davidson.com

ago to achieve its present ascendancy with about three million sales a year worldwide. It also tops the sales league for 650cc plus bikes in Japan, the backyard of its major competitors. The company's net income rose 45% from 2001 to 2005 to represent almost half the heavyweight motorcycle market in the USA. Its secret? 'We fulfill dreams through the experience of motorcycling.'[10] Now that puts the company into a rather special brand space.

The evolving role of brands

For a maker of ruggedly designed and beefily engineered machines to depict itself in the dream-fulfilment business may no longer be so surprising now that brands have graduated from product differentiation to the customer experience era. What is more significant is that the power of this insight inspired Harley to generate a host of new business development ideas that it arguably would never have spotted. This is a far cry from the origins of branding. Early on it was mainly about establishing ownership. As every devotee of Westerns knows, branding was used to differentiate otherwise identical herds of cattle with a unique ranch symbol. The clear message was: Hands off. If you couldn't resist the temptation to rustle someone else's cattle, then the Lazy S or other distinctive mark burnt into the animal's hide was a bit of a give away when you came to

---

[10] http://www.harley-davidson.com

track them down. In the consumer era, brands still fulfil the identity and ownership definition roles. But the difference between their use in the Wild West and the contemporary commercial world is that their purpose is to attract rather than warn off. Today, brands are used to send a whole set of messages.

The evolution in the role of brands continues to be driven by all the factors identified in the marketplace and business environment. Above all, though, it has been the constant need for suppliers to set themselves apart from the competition, a job that has become more difficult as time goes by.

Once brands became a means of differentiating products in the consumer marketplace, they started to operate with increasing sophistication. In the early phase of branding, the focus was differentiation through product features. Once everyone was shouting similar messages, the next place for brands to go involved promoting consumer benefits. When pushing attributes of this kind no longer had the same cutting edge, the race was on to differentiate companies by values. More recently, the competitive battleground has moved on to differentiation through memorable consumer experience.

Go into an Apple store and there is no escaping the intensity with which the company sets out to put across the brand experience. For more companies, the emphasis is on making an indelible and positive impression on the customer. Enter Swatch's New York store and you are surrounded by the mechanism of a watch. Or visit Guinness in Dublin and find yourself in the simulation of a giant glass. These are some of the ways in which companies are consciously making the brand come alive for the consumer. So brand history has seen more and different roles layered on brands as companies search for the prizes of growing sales and customer loyalty.

These are some of the key ways in which brands are used today.

Ownership and identity. Trademarks and logos are the contemporary equivalent of the Lazy S and enable brands to be legally defensible. They are a come-on signal for customers and send a stay-away message to competitors.

Product identification. In crowded markets packed with me-too products, distinctive brands help consumers to single out one company's product from the herd.

Corporate values. It is not only products that can be branded. Organisations, too, are brands in their own right that have distinctive features and attributes. Where a brand stands on issues ranging from animal product testing to global warming and social responsibility has moved centre stage for many sectors.

Apple stores set out to distil the brand experience

Employer branding. More recently, companies have realised that the marketplace represents just one brand audience. Equally important are employees who need to buy into the company proposition and values. Incidentally, the same goes for other key stakeholders in the business.

Marketplace positioning. Brands can be used to fine-tune a company's positioning in the marketplace using a range of sponsorship, advertising and marketing techniques.

Unique selling point, USP. Part of the differentiation that companies need to establish is what exactly sets them apart from the competition. In the past, brands have striven to achieve a unique selling proposition through design, technology or matchless price/performance. With a proliferation of choice, this kind of differentiation has become tougher to achieve and invariably short-lived. The battle has moved to a new plane.

Tribal identity. Gucci shoes, Armani suits, Mont Blanc pens are as synonymous with Wall Street as derivatives and insider trading. On the streets, it could be Nike trainers. Flash the brand and join the club.

Safety and insurance. Gaining a safe-as-houses reputation, or one which puts you above criticism, can be a winner. Volvo's traditional emphasis on safety before the auto industry picked up on this consumer concern more widely gave the carmaker an edge. No one got fired for buying IBM was an old maxim in information technology circles for those who wanted a trouble-free, if unexciting, life.

Personal statement. For other segments of the market, it is not running with the herd but standing out from the crowd. Brands that can say 'Look at me, I've got my own style' put themselves in niche company.

Lifestyle. Brands enable people to make a personal statement identifying them as followers of a particular lifestyle. Apple and Harley Davidson have pulled this off with strong brands that are associated with preferences for independence and nonconformity.

Strategy and business development. The brand can become a vehicle for plotting the future development of a business – providing it is richly and comprehensively defined and understood in the first place.

Innovation. It is not only brand extensions and the development of new categories that can be spun out of a strong brand. There is also plenty of potential for building on their intrinsic attributes and features to develop new products and services.

These are just some of the ways in which brands play a central part in marketing but also in driving business growth and development, and the brand story is still evolving as smart companies look beyond traditional and conventional marketing applications into other areas of the business. It is not so much a matter of developing a brand strategy as a brand-led strategy for the business.

It means that brands are layered with significance. For example, what kind of company lies behind the brand is becoming as important as the products themselves. One thing is certain, as brand significance blurs across corporate, cultural and market borders, failing to manage every aspect of the brand looks increasingly perilous. That job starts with establishing exactly what it stands for.

Putting corporate values on the line

While the methods companies use to establish their corporate and organisational credentials are slicker and more sophisticated than in the past, some businesses were early to sense the need to persuade customers that they were in tune with the prevailing attitudes of the times. Check out this advertisement placed by the Triumph cycle maker in the early twentieth century. Its claims would have the company in the dock for flagrant prejudice today. But when it appeared in the early 1900s, the Triumph Cycle Company would have argued that it was just appealing to its target customers' beliefs. Under the heading 'Male or female labour', its advertisement said:

'The male mechanic in the Workshop has proved himself infinitely superior to the female – he is capable of doing better, more exact, more reliable work.

Morally, mixed labour does not raise the standard of either worker, and considerably lowers the standard of the work produced.

Triumph Cycles are made in a factory where no female labour whatever is employed. Female labour and best work do not go together, therefore let your machine be a Triumph. The Best Bicycle British Workmanship can produce and made by skilled male mechanics only.'[11]

There you have it: buy one of our cycles and buy into our corporate philosophy. Whether or not Triumph had thought through the implications of alienating the female half of the population, it was a clear attempt to identify its brand with a specific set of corporate values. More recently, the principle that the brand should encapsulate key attributes of the company has taken on fresh significance, although for rather different and more enlightened reasons than this early attempt at corporate values branding.

Body Shop, one of the leading champions of ethical business, made the way in which it manufactured its products,

[11] *From Dynasties to Dotcoms*, Carol Kennedy, Director Publications, 2003.

57

dealt with its suppliers and ran its operations an integral part of its brand story. When you choose Body Shop products, you buy into a set of principles and a well-defined vision of what the business stands for. The multilayered brand stands for a portfolio of product, production and business values. All successful brands have discovered a knack for doing this. The problem is that for every stellar brand there are thousands that have yet to discover their unique potential in brand terms. Or to exploit that in all the ways that this brand consciousness enables.

Seeing is believing: opening the doors of perception

Anyone who wants to take their use of brands to a new level has plenty to think about. There are techniques derived from sociology and psychology that can be used to explore the impact of brands on consumer behaviour as well as to probe the drivers and motivators that shape buying patterns. There are also plenty of insights from these disciplines to help brand builders understand the possible results of their efforts. Some of these findings provide a healthy antidote to the assumption that brand building is achieved by beaming out the right images and messages.

Psychology tells us that what we 'see' is the product of a cocktail of influences. Gender, age, values, beliefs, our assumptions, emotions, culture, even mind-altering drugs all help to determine how we interpret our perception of the world around us. Whether or not we are aware of it, there is a kind of mental alchemy going on inside our heads that makes the act of seeing a highly personal and complex phenomenon. And the feedback loop between image, memory, feelings, experience and attitudes is constantly being modified. As a brand creator, how confident can you be that consumers are on your brand wavelength?

Whether McDonald's golden arches conjure up an image of yummy burgers and fries or super-saturated junk food will vary from one individual to another, from child to parent, across cultures and depending on personal beliefs and prejudices. Orchestrating people's perceptions of a brand is no simple task, particularly when the messages are multilayered.

There is also the whole mystery of the power of brands to influence our judgement. Most people would like to think that when they say they prefer brand A to brand B this is the result of a conscious, informed process. But whether it is their reason, emotions or other senses that shape opinions is not always so simple to untangle. The whole dark process has been the subject of a number of tests and investigations. Remember the famous Pepsi challenge?

With the constant rivalry between Coca-Cola and Pepsi Cola, any shift in market share has always been a cause for celebration or concern, depending on which way the scales tipped. Back in the 1970s, exclusive Coke and Pepsi drinkers accounted for 18% and 4%, respectively of the soft drinks market. By the 1980s, the comparable figures were 12% and 11%. Pepsi was convinced that it was the unique flavour of their cola that lay behind its rise in popularity. To prove its point, Pepsi staged blind tastings of the two rival drinks in shopping malls and other forums. Without knowing which was which, shoppers were invited to try both and say which they preferred. The trial results vindicated Pepsi's hunch: 57% chose their cola over the 47% who preferred Coke. Televised ad campaigns based on the experiment opened up a whole new chapter in brand promotion. It also sparked renewed competition between Pepsi and Coca-Cola.

But that is not the end of the story. Fast forward to 2003 and consider the results of a set of experiments that used brain scanner technology to look at what goes on in people's heads in these kinds of trials.

When subjects took the same blind tasting test, their neural activity was measured and their reactions showed that the group was more or less equally divided in their preference for Coke and Pepsi. But when they were told which brand they were drinking, the neural response patterns showed that three-quarters preferred Coca-Cola. It was evidence of the brand effect in action.[12]

---

[12] 'Coca Cola or Pepsi – The voice of the brain', GCRM White Paper, 2006, www.gcrm.com

While this validation of the impact of brand on experience provides a major boost to those who believe in the power of brands, replicating the high-tech test conditions is not exactly a practical proposition. But blind tests, rather like the Pepsi challenge, reveal a similar result. Sampson Lee, the author of 'Coca Cola or Pepsi – The voice of the brain', presented university students with a similar choice. The two-part experiment involved two tastings: one where they were told which of the two they were drinking, the second being a blind tasting. Although many were either Coke or Pepsi fans, up to half were inconsistent and confused the taste when they did not know which was which.

Although neuromarketing is in its infancy, continuing experiments at Carnegie Mellon and other universities are adding to our understanding of the impact of advertising and promotion on customer behaviour. Already mind reading is starting to illuminate the way in which pleasure, pain, gratification and other reactions are mirrored in brain activity. It is a short step to applying these techniques to explore the way consumers react to different brands and products.

According to UC Berkeley neuroscientist Robert Knight, a scientific adviser to NeuroFocus, three trends have converged to create neuromarketing:

'... a better understanding of the regions of the brain; precise sensors to measure when, say, the memory centre is active; and software to infer from these telltale signs whether a given message resonated with men or women of different ages.

Neuroscience today is where physics was at the turn of the last century. We've had the groundbreaking thoughts and theories. Now we are measuring and testing.'[13]

What was long believed to be the case is now being confirmed by research: brands really do get inside your head and influence your preferences.

Dysfunctional brand management: the search for a cure

Other factors have brought new issues for brand builders. Over time, companies have realised that brands have relevance to all stakeholder groups, not just customers and prospects, but business partners and those who work inside the organisation. Engaging everyone who works for the business makes sense not just because you want people to understand what the brand is all about, but also because

---

[13] 'Coming to a marketer near you: Brain scanning', Tom Abate, *San Francisco Chronicle*, 19th May 2008.

they individually contribute to the overall behaviour of the brand. Nike's restructuring around divisions focused on individual sports, which means that it recruits people who think, act and behave like the customers they are trying to excite about the company's products. Google wants to attract engineers who are web enthusiasts and ready to keep working on their own ideas.

More than that, without that shared, internal organisational empathy and understanding, any work on the brand is likely to be built on shaky foundations. At the most obvious level, the absence of a well-grounded concept of the brand means that marketing and advertising become hit or miss. Worse still, brand confusion makes well-focused product development and innovation impossible. It is like trying to assemble a complex jigsaw without any vision of the picture you are trying to piece together: the results will be random and aimless.

The approach of most companies to brand management does them few favours in this respect. Our motivation as brand consultants for developing an alternative approach was the growing frustration with the widespread failure to make the most of brands and the resulting difficulties we experienced in working with companies struggling with the fall-out from dysfunctional brand management. The diagnosis was simple. Most companies were not able to manage their brands in a comprehensive, inside-out way that enabled them to put their energy into well-focused business growth and innovation. At that stage we could describe the goal: the development of a well-grounded, consistent and shared understanding of the spirit of the brand. But we were a long way from finding the answers.

Try this self-assessment test to gauge the present status of your brand.

- When was the last time you reviewed the status of your brand, its strengths, weaknesses and potential for development (and what conclusions did you reach)?
- Which change drivers in the marketplace and business environment represent the biggest threats and opportunities for your brand?
- How is your brand affected by major trends in your marketplace, from the rise of globalisation to the Internet?
- What are the biggest risks to the integrity of your brand and how would you counter them?
- Which of the several roles listed in this chapter does your brand currently fulfil and how would you rate its performance in each area?
- Does your organisation treat your brand as a business asset?
- In what ways do you maximise brand value to your organisation – internally as well as externally?

- What impact has the shift of power to consumers had on your brand reputation and do you have a strategy for managing this?
- How well is your brand aligned with corporate strategy?
- How satisfied are you that the spirit of your brand is understood and reflected in the culture of the organisation?

ENDURING MYTHS

NEW CHALLENGES
AND REALITIES

Chapter 3

'Today, branding is everything – and I mean everything. Brands are not simply products or services. Brands are the sum total of all the images that people have in their heads about a particular company and a particular mark.'[14]

Scott Bedbury, CEO of Brandstream, a Seattle-based marketing consultancy, formerly worldwide advertising director, Nike and chief marketing officer, Starbucks

This chapter looks at some lingering myths that limit the horizons of brand thinking and creativity. It summarises a number of the most serious blocks to the effective use of brand power and the new realities that are shaping today's opportunities. The evolution of brand power over time has been a story of changing business and market conditions, as well as growing sophistication in the way brands have been developed and deployed. The problem has been that while some companies have been in the vanguard of responding to the threats and opportunities thrown up by new circumstances, many more companies are handicapped by outdated

---

[14] 'Brand New Branding', Fast Company, July 2001.

and obsolete brand management practices. They are prisoners of the past.

From our wide experience of working with many different companies in different sectors, these are all-too-common symptoms of underperforming brands.

Myth One: Brands are just about differentiation in the marketplace

If you think this, then you will never lift yourself from the fourth division of brand performance. This narrow view massively underplays your brand's potential for driving the business forward and is likely to be the product of a mindset associated with those who see brands in the narrowest marketing context. Your brand can spearhead your strategy, business development and fortunes as an organisation. You need look no further than big-brand thinkers like Apple to see the traction from aligning the whole business behind the brand.

Myth Two: What you see is all you get

Logos, trademarks and design values may be essential for the brand to be communicated to the world at large. But these are only visible symbols of what should be a much larger and deeper set of brand attributes that these symbols represent. Aside from anything else, limiting branding to superficial product differentiation means that companies are missing out on developing the brand experience or making connections with their customers at the values and emotional levels. The first step is to put in the work to develop a shared understanding of the spirit of the brand and then ensure that it is lived by the company before figuring out how to communicate this bigger brand experience into the marketplace.

Myth Three: Brands only concern the marketing department

While marketing and brand managers play a central role in ensuring that brands are properly planned, promoted and developed to ensure that products and services flourish in the marketplace, this is only part of it. We have entered a new chapter in the evolution of brand management. The practice, launched as a result of Neil McElroy's famous 1931 memo which first established brand management as a discipline inside Procter & Gamble, went on to change marketing everywhere. But recent developments in the role of brands, the way they are managed and the marketplace have redrawn the rules. Brands now concern a much wider corporate community than just the marketing department and call for a more inclusive approach.

There is a danger that a siloed approach to brand management – it can all be left to marketing – leads to a breakdown in communication between marketing, new product development and other sections of the organisation that undermines the realisation of brand objectives.

The way to avoid this danger is to ensure that there is proper 360-degree involvement and communication between all brand stakeholders in the company. A wise solution, but one that is often overlooked in large, bureaucratic and functionally structured organisations.

Outside the brand management environment, everyone from the CEO, the ultimate owner of the brand, to the receptionist has a shared responsibility for the brand's performance and behaviour. Raising corporate consciousness of the spirit of the brand, and the potential positive and negative implications of individual actions, statements and behaviour, is the way to minimise the risks here.

Myth Four: Customers are the only brand consumers that count

This is a dangerously limited view. Many other groups, including partners and investors, have a significant influence on corporate performance in their own way, and their attitudes and perception of the organisation should be carefully managed. How they perceive your business is just as crucial. Ensuring that the brand is well defined for all these other stakeholders should be part of the larger marketing programme. Remember that a brand needs to pass the authenticity and trust tests for these people as well. Which means that there is no point in projecting a superficial gloss. People have got to be convinced that you are as good as your image.

Myth Five: External research will tell you all you need to know about your brand

Focus groups, market research, analysts' reports and other investigative methods can tell you a great deal of valuable information. But they cannot make up for a lack of insight into the genius of the brand. Market research will tell you what the outside world thinks. But the market cannot do your thinking for you. The brand, in the sense that it is defined in this book, can only be determined by the organisation itself. Experiencing your brand, much as your customers do, can help you to get beneath the surface. But that is only part of the experiential journey you need to take to plumb the brand's deeper secrets and achieve actionable insights.

Myth Six: You can bury the bad news

This may have been easier in the past, but there are now no hiding places. As a consumer, you had little chance of finding an independent evaluation of a brand. Aside from the Consumer Association, specialist magazines and a few campaigning consumer champions like Ralph Nader, there were relatively few opportunities for discovering how brands were rated in the marketplace or where they were failing the consumer. Now the web is heaving with opportunities to find out what other customers think of your business, with industry-specific sites that carry reviews and comments. In a less structured but still influential way, social networks provide a forum for people to share their thoughts, fears and suspicions about everything – including the companies they work for. There is always a website that will reveal what people inside and outside your walls think of your company's brand and products. With the constantly growing rash of blogs, consumer reviews and forums, it is impossible to suppress consumer comment, as Ryanair's abortive efforts to shut down complaints websites about the airline showed.

Not surprisingly, some companies have decided it would be better to join the bloggers rather than fight them, although sneaky attempts to plant fake blogs can turn out to be counter-productive. The Consumerist[15] and Adrants[16] are two sites that have covered the implications of these practices.

Soon, rather than just receiving a ticking off, anyone from authors posing as readers and giving themselves five-star ratings on Amazon through to major consumer brand names doing the same kind of thing, could find themselves on

---

[15] http://consumerist.com/
[16] http://adrants.com/

the receiving end of a prosecution under new European Union legislation. The questions for marketing departments tempted to post fake blogs or spurious network contributions is whether they still end up losing in the end when any fleeting victories are overwhelmed by the waves of adverse comments. As an act of brand building, it does not make much sense.

It may not be quite the kind of transparency that companies would always welcome, but the worldwide web creates a new challenge for those who care about the integrity of their brands. Massaging the facts, or burying bad news in the hope that only the good will get out, does not work. Another sobering thought. Unlike the world of print, when it can be a physical slog to dig out the facts from past or scarce publications, once on the web, nothing is further than a click away. And once logged, anything that has been posted is there for keeps and as accessible tomorrow as it is today.

Myth Seven: With the internationalisation of markets, it is easy for brands to act globally

The answer is only sometimes. Even then, it depends how skilfully brand globalisation is handled.

Think global, act local. Not only has Walls' long-running use of the jingle 'Just one Cornetto ...' weathered the test of time.

The product has proved to have staying power and cross-border appeal. As far as the consumer is concerned, there may be only one Cornetto. What they are unaware of is the fact that there are dozens of product variations formulated to meet the ice-cream tastes of different nations. It is one example of how to take a universal proposition and then localise it.

Whether brands can successfully succeed globally is down to a number of factors. The trouble is that there will always be a strong temptation to force fit a global brand into a specific market with the minimum of localisation. When a brand attempts to bludgeon its way through the world's markets making minimum concessions to local conditions, any economies of scale this is meant to achieve tend to be illusory. It means ending up with the lowest rather than the highest common denominators.

Key to finding the right answer lies in assessing the spirit of the brand. It may be that it is globally consistent and readily transferable across borders. As brands, Starbucks works as well in London as New York, or McDonald's in Pennsylvania or Paris. By contrast, the US car industry has struggled to bring its marques to Europe. With only a few notable exceptions, like the Jeep, the American brand is not an asset. In most cases, it has been an uphill struggle. For General Motors, success through localisation means using a local brand, like Vauxhall in the UK. Sometimes, it can be easier to globalise new brands that do not have the same baggage or legacy as older, established brands.

Challenge One: Do you confuse new product development and innovation with brand extension?

There are few more effective ways of amplifying business success than extending the brand into complementary products and services that offer something novel to existing customers and draw in new fans. But that is quite different from tinkering with the size, shape or make-up of an existing product. The problem for some companies is that they run up against an innovation barrier where this is all they can do in the absence of a better answer.

This need not be the fate of companies with even old, well-established brands. Discovering, or reformulating, the spirit of the brand can remove the innovation block and enable the business to envisage genuine opportunities for brand extensions rather than modifications.

Challenge Two: Do you think that you are the real owner of your brand?

This is not such a daft question as it sounds. Of course the company is the legal owner of trademarks, logos and so on. At other levels, ownership may not be so obvious. A powerful ad agency can assume a disproportionate influence on the brand and start to lead the client by the nose. This is a recipe for client frustration and maybe some loss of control. The brand is often the real loser.

Or are the real owners the consumers? The power of consumers can be enormous. In the Internet era, the reality is that consumers can constantly exert their influence on the brand through their comments, recommendations and word-of-mouse postings. In pre-web days it was easier for companies to become remote from consumers. Today, their in-your-face response makes it more or less impossible for brand builders to ignore consumer reactions. Also, witness the brand hijacking episodes in the histories of upmarket companies Burberry and Ralph Lauren featured in Chapter Two.

Other external stakeholders can also make their influence felt. One potentially powerful agent in the brand control equation is the lobby group. In many sectors, the credentials of an environmentally or socially responsible brand can be shattered by the publicity given to claims of non-green or responsible practices. It happened to Shell over the disposal of a North Sea oil platform and to Nike with the controversy over child labour in the Far East.

Although there can be no guarantee of immunity from the impact of third-party actions, ensuring that brand values are embedded in the way the company behaves across all sections of the organisation is a first step to avoiding disasters.

Challenge Three: Is your brand development two paces behind the competition?

Some companies take three years, some take three months, while the fleet of foot take three weeks to respond to new threats and opportunities. In whichever sector you operate, it is a fair bet that life is moving fast, and accelerating. Whether you are an established maker of cars, electric drills or clothes, the competition is likely to be coming in cheaper, from all directions and probably just as good in quality terms as the home-grown variety. These are testing times for any brand caught up in the rush of global competition.

Ironically, while our instant communications network means that the air will be buzzing with up-to-the-minute news about the latest developments, the corporate machine takes far longer to lurch into action. Redefining the spirit of the brand, especially its behaviour and a new-found passion for rapid performance, will move the organisation into a higher gear. Otherwise, prepare to go the way of the traditional Swiss watch industry.

Challenge Four: Do you still believe you have a unique selling point?

Not so long ago, every brand manager believed that they had to stand or fall on product differentiation. Unless market-ers could claim that 'We are the only one whose product ...'

they were likely to fret that they were not in the game. Today, any claim of uniqueness is almost certainly destined to be a five-minute wonder. Instant me-too imitations, or leapfrogging improvements from a competitor, have made this an unwinnable contest. This has been a fact of life in FMCG markets for many years, but it is also a feature of other sectors, from software and sports equipment to retail brands.

Starbucks might have made the first move, but Costa Coffee and Café Nero were hard on their heels in the high streets of the world. Harley Davidson's macho bike style has been mimicked by Yamaha and other Japanese look-alikes. Unchallenged for decades, like so many traditional sectors, Western musical instrument makers were unassailable until the past few decades. Now whether you want a Fender Stratocaster sound-alike, or a grand piano that stands comparison with a Steinway, you can find a close match from a Far Eastern source. The world is awash with products that compete head-on in terms of features, price and performance. So what enables brands to set themselves apart in this world of super abundance?

There may be very little to choose between one product and another as far as price, performance or features, but there can still be something which consumers find unique. Brands that project an intangible quality to do with the values and genius of the brand have more chance of success.

The answer has to do with the brand experience. Uniqueness has moved from the realms of the physical to the metaphysical. Establishing something special about the brand experience, or communicating a brand dream that catches the imagination, means that you can still stand out from the crowd.

The new rules of brand engagement

One of the significant trends over the past couple of decades has been the development of the brand as a unifying principle in business. This is reflected in all sorts of ways, not least in the adoption of the language of brands by anyone who feels they have a story to tell and a message to get across. Many political parties have taken branding to heart, to the extent that they go to great lengths to ensure that their policies are packaged and presented to the electorate in a way that ensures they are consistently on-message.

Increasingly, companies are seen as brands in their own right. This allows, for example, major retailers such as Wal-Mart, M&S and Tesco to position themselves in the marketplace with identities, values and market positioning that can be dissected much like those of the products they sell. Nor is it just retailers that are now branded: the same goes for businesses and organisations of all types that have seized on the possibility of putting their brand to work. So infectious has brand consciousness become that it has influenced thinking far beyond business. It is commonly used by political parties, sports teams, charities and celebrities to manage their image and development. Why stop there? Once you start seeing the transferable properties in branding, then the principle can be applied universally, right down to individual level. As Tom Peters argued, everyone is CEO of Me Inc.

'You're every bit as much a brand as Nike, Coke, Pepsi, or the Body Shop. To start thinking like your own favourite brand manager, ask yourself the same question the brand managers at Nike, Coke, Pepsi, or the Body Shop ask themselves: What is it that my product or service does that makes it different?'[17]

Ironically, it can be easier for a determined individual to implement the range of smart development practices that Peters recommends than for an organisation. There are no functional barriers in the way, there are no arguments about roles and responsibilities, there is unity of purpose. These are luxuries that organisations do not enjoy.

Here are some of the new rules of engagement that enable you to transcend the legacy of the lingering myths that we dealt with above.

---

[17] 'The Brand Called You', Tom Peters, Fast Company, 18th December 2007.

Rule One: Brands are too important to be left to the brand manager

It may command all the paraphernalia of brand management but when brand management has been exclusively pigeon-holed as a functional responsibility, a company can struggle to get full value from the brand. While excellence in day-to-day brand management is a prerequisite, it represents only part of the job. Just because marketing is on the case, does not mean that the rest of the organisation can relax and forget about its share of brand responsibilities. The delegate-and-dump approach is dangerous for several reasons.

First, it undermines the brand as a powerhouse for strategic innovation and business development. That really does require joined up thinking across the business at every level.

Second, it can disenfranchise everyone else from taking their share of responsibility for maintaining the integrity of the brand. Everyone plays a role as a brand ambassador, whatever their position in the enterprise when they talk to customers, partners, suppliers, potential employees and members of the community.

Third, the view that someone somewhere in a dedicated department is looking after the brand may mean that the business as a whole becomes complacent or careless in ways that can be damaging to brand performance. It is not just the fact that positive messages are not spread about the brand; the results of unguarded or thoughtless comments can be far more serious in their consequences.

Fourth, it can lead to the disassociation of brand from strategy. If senior managers and policy-makers do not share a passionate understanding of the brand, then big decisions may fail to build the business and undermine its performance.

Rule Two: Brands need to be reviewed and renewed

Tell tale signs of underperforming brands include loss of touch with customers, failure to keep pace with marketplace trends, general tiredness and a lack of buzz. The longer established the brand, the greater the need for constant renewal.

Getting to super-brand status can be tough. But staying at the top is even tougher, as the trajectories of some once great but faltering brands reveal. Marks & Spencer's fall from favour as the high street retailer par excellence is a salutary lesson that companies forget about the essence of their brands at their peril. Yet, as the company demonstrated, being down does not necessarily mean that you are out. Its return to winning ways is charted in Chapter Seven, in a closer analysis of its brand performance over the years. Nor is M&S the only company to concede a position of apparent unassailable domination. Others have lost their way and slipped down the rankings, only to claw their way back with considerable difficulty.

When Disney decided to focus on action movies in the 1990s, its box office success suffered until it reverted to its traditional strategy of majoring on film animation. Harley Davidson hauled itself back from unprofitable diversions and rediscovered its mission as an iconic manufacturer of easy rider motorcycles. Both companies, as we explain later, could probably have avoided their strategic drift if they had paid closer attention to the spirit of their brand.

There are plenty of examples where companies have had to reinvent their brands to remain competitive. Not so long ago, Skoda cars were lampooned for their chronic unreliability. But under Volkswagen's ownership, the byword for poor engineering has been salvaged to the extent that the marque now receives car-of-the-year awards.

Rule Three: The leader is the brand

It is not always possible to prevent a brand going belly up. There are some infamous examples of how reputation and standing have been destroyed overnight by an unguarded comment by the person at the top.

One of the most well known cases of a brand disaster was Gerald Ratner's 1991 speech at the Institute of Directors' annual convention. He joked that one of his firm's products was 'total crap' and pointed out that some of its earrings were 'cheaper than a prawn sandwich'. The CEO's apparent contempt for his firm's products, and by implication his customers' tastes, was a gift to journalists looking for a juicy story. But the markets did not find it so amusing. About £500m was wiped from the company's value overnight.

Ratner's prawn-sandwich gaffe is a reminder that brand reputation can be a fragile commodity. It also underlines how important a leader's public statements can be on supporting or puncturing that reputation. The impact of his unguarded comments confirms that a brand's reputation can be highly volatile, has enormous influence on corporate value and has a relevance to all sections of a company's stakeholders.

Ironically, there was nothing different about Ratner's jewellery the day before he made his private opinions public, or the day after the IoD event. The products were neither better nor worse as a result of what was said. What was different was that the brand's credibility had been disastrously holed below the water line. Imagine, for a moment, that the boss had done the usual thing and puffed his products' value-for-money appeal instead of rubbishing them. Customers' perceptions would have been unruffled and they would have continued to buy Ratner's jewellery. No one in the City would have batted an eyelid. He may even have added a point or two to the share price. Instead, Gerald Ratner succeeded in demolishing City confidence in himself, the brand and the business for what turned out to be anything but a cheap laugh. In retrospect, his misjudgement can be seen for what it was: an act of unthinking public brandicide.

This episode is a salutary reminder of how closely the CEO is identified with a company's brand. When the top executive speaks at a major forum like the annual IoD convention, people take notice. On occasions such as these, it is the brand that is speaking.

This is not a principle that you need to explain to Richard Branson, who epitomises Virgin and has made the promotion of the brand his own personal crusade. His open-neck shirt and casual informality marked him out as a maverick in a world of grey-suits. That, as well as an endless appetite for indulging in publicity stunts and a succession of derring-do adventures, has earned him, and Virgin, celebrity status. The net result is that Branson and Virgin are synonymous and rarely far from the headlines. He ranks alongside a handful of CEOs who play the leader-as-brand principle to perfection. Branson also has unshakable faith in brand power: 'I believe there is almost no limit to what a brand can do, but only if it is used properly.'[18]

---

[18] *Dream Merchants & Howboys*, Barry Gibbons, Capstone, 2004.

It is not only in the world of business that the brand/reputation interplay operates. The same set of dynamics applies to any kind of organisation that relies on a strong public appeal. Politicians of all colours in every continent have taken the concept of branding to heart and know all too well that leadership and electability go together.

The continuing travails of the Labour Party show the inextricable link between leader and brand. Although Tony Blair may have been running low in the trust and credibility stakes before he handed over the prime ministership in 2007, his difficulties look trivial compared to the depths of Gordon Brown's problems. The Labour brand has received a series of body blows. Back-bench revolts over the withdrawal of the 10% tax band. The drubbing administered by voters in the local elections of spring 2008 marked a 40-year low in Labour fortunes. As a leader, Gordon Brown's standing has continued to plummet along with that of the Labour Party.

Many on the back benches believe that some of the worst problems could have been avoided if the government had not turned its back on what the party regarded as core principles, particularly the abandonment of the 10% tax band that affects the least well off. Looked at from the brand dream perspective, Labour would have seemed to have ignored its roots, failed to find a new vision and behaved in a way that has caused widespread outrage among the party faithful. Whichever way you look at it, it faces a long climb back.

By contrast, the benefits from having a leader who personifies the brand creates wholly different performance conditions. There is no one that Apple fans would rather see than Steve Jobs unveiling the latest product at a MacWorld convention, for example. Charismatic leaders who live and breathe the brand, especially those who are the business founders, give their brands a huge advantage. Those leaders who have forgotten what made the brand great in the first place, or worse still never really developed a passionate commitment, often do untold damage.

Rule Four: Brand reputation may not be easily quantifiable, but it is a major asset

From the closing decades of the twentieth century onwards, the issue of how corporate value should be calculated has been subject to intense debate. For some time it has been clear that the yawning gap between book and market valuations called for explanation and quantification. The problem has been that accounting for the difference has proved notoriously tricky. As the stuff of the knowledge era, intellectual capital, market share, reputation, skills and not least brands all belong on the intangibles balance sheet. The snag is putting a value on them.

Notwithstanding that difficulty, marketing people have understood the value of brands for many years, even if precise valuation has foxed accountants. It has also stood Warren

Buffet, one of the world's richest men, in good stead. His Berkshire Hathaway group has amassed a fortune by buying up and harvesting brands.

Meanwhile Interbrand, one of the leaders in brand valuation, has developed its own method of valuing brands that is in line with accounting principles. This quantified approach contrasts with the often subjective methods used for measuring knowledge and other components in the intangibles range. Underpinning Interbrand's formula is a valuation based on future cash flow.

The three-stage approach starts with estimating how much of a company's income is attributable to brands based on research into how influential the brand is in purchasing decisions as opposed to other factors such as availability. This provides the basis for calculating cash flow over time.

Second, the brand's strength is assessed against seven criteria: the market in which it operates, stability and loyalty, leadership in its sector, long-term trends, support and investment, geographic scope and degree of protection. This generates a brand strength score that takes into account future threats to its earning potential.

Third, a brand valuation based on the outcome of the preceding phases. Finally, the exercise culminates in a brand report.

The method has been used for valuing product brands and corporate brands, and in a wide range of industries including service industries and financial services.

Although the heartland of the world of brands may have been the consumer sectors, brand value is increasingly figuring in industrial sector thinking.

While this method can reckon a brand's value in terms of future revenue, there are other more pragmatic reasons for taking the brand value proposition seriously. Examples like Ratner make it clear that there is nothing insubstantial about the financial implications of destroying a brand's credibility. It can be counted in terms of customer spend, analysts' ratings, stock market performance and competitive clout. In some cases like this, also the ruin of the business. An asset in its own right, a strong brand is nothing less than an index of future corporate performance. Undermine the brand and you may, like Ratner, be left without so much as the price of a prawn sandwich.

Rule Five: Your brand should be one of the most important drivers of performance at every level of the business

One of the most important premises for this book is that the brand dream has to infuse the whole organisation. It is not something that should be locked up in the minds of a few brand managers or senior executives. Its power derives from being universally shared. Unless that happens, then the potential for influencing performance for the better will never be tapped.

The journey has to start with total immersion in the genius of the brand, its values, strengths, weaknesses and the way it influences corporate behaviour. This provides the inspiration to jumpstart innovation and new business development. The spirit of the brand can then become a guiding principle for strategy and future growth. That includes projecting it faithfully into the marketplace and public domain. It also promotes engagement inside the organisation, shapes culture and behaviour.

Rule Six: Get in touch with the genius of the brand to discover its transformational power

Back to the super brands. Attempts to explain their success invariably result in a search for a simple, neat formula. Is their secret a market-beating product or service? Or sheer marketing brilliance? Superior brand management? Great market research? An unrivalled customer proposition? Superb customer service? Invariably, it is all of these things, but also so much more.

In almost every case, someone, usually the founder, had a dream of what they wanted to achieve and this was what drove the business and its success. That dream became their Pole star. The vitality of the dream determines the vitality of the company. Look at Apple. Under its founders, the company took off big time. Later, with the departure of the chief dreamers, its performance dipped and the business lost its momentum and performance suffered. After the return of Steve Jobs, the company found a new dream that gave it second wind. The genius of the Apple brand was rediscovered and reapplied to spark a new wave of innovation with the launch of its consumer electronics products as well as a new wave of computers.

Unless you see your brand as an expression of the underlying dream that inspires your organisation, then the enterprise is unlikely to realise its potential. Communicating that dream so that it makes sense and enthuses customers and others from analysts to shareholders, partners, the public, the community and, not least, employees is an essential part of the job. Every touch point from the receptionist and delivery department through to service and sales. Brand value is amplified or diminished with every interaction with these groups. And what the chief executive says to the media, conferences and every other public platform can have huge ramifications for brand standing.

Get in touch with the current status of your brand

These are some of the most important myths, challenges and new rules for tuning into brand power. See how your organisation measures up to this checklist. Start the internal process of discovery that should flush out the issues that matter most. What you find out as a result of that review should tell you a lot about your current brand strategy, along with its deficiencies and the scope for taking it to a higher level.

On the basis of working with major brands and organisations over the past two decades, it is clear that conventional approaches get conventional results. The answer is to become more intuitive, less judgemental and more creative in engaging with your brand. You cannot think your way to insights. This is something that needs both right- and left-brain collaboration, which is why the brand dream method draws on a number of traditions, ancient and modern, to create a method for the third millennium that gets to the answers that other techniques fail to produce. How the process and the model work are covered in more detail later on in Chapters Four and Five.

how the

BRAND DREAM

process took shape

chapter 4

'Dreams are today's answers to tomorrow's questions.'

Edgar Cayce

The story so far. The previous chapters have unfolded the big issues, including the nature and development of brands and their continuing evolution as a business asset. However you choose to read the trends in the growth of consumer influence and the stories of brand hijacking and value dilution, they contain some clear messages:

- Outside your organisation, brands have a life of their own.
- You can influence, but not always control, what happens to your brand in the marketplace.
- You mess with the core values of your brand at your peril.

All of which leads to a number of big questions:

- How can you best protect your brand's integrity?
- How can you build brand value in unpredictable times?
- How can you keep the dream alive?

These were issues that were never far from my mind in all the assignments that we undertook for clients. The conviction that there had to be a better way of solving these and other brand challenges was growing. A number of ideas started to coalesce.

All the strategies that are deployed in managing your brand are useless unless it has been possible to fathom the underlying forces that shape the make-up of your brand. This had to be the starting point for protecting the brand's integrity and the only sure foundation for making inspired decisions about innovation, future development and effective promotion. It would also help to avoid the mistakes that can lead to brand disasters. If there were a modern marketing version of the Delphic Oracle's rubric, the threshold would bear the inscription, 'Know Thy Brand'. Inside every brand there should be a compelling story, a dream of possibilities and values that represent a strategic compass for the business. There were also other criteria that any solution would have to address.

The inside story of the brand needed to be made public and shared widely, not just within the marketing department but amongst everyone from the chief executive to the person who answers the phone and drives the delivery truck. The challenge was how to develop a common understanding of what makes the brand special at every level of the organisation in a way that was relevant and meaningful. The secret had to be revealed in ways that staff can relate to.

Market surveys, balance sheets, brand value accounting and statistical analysis did not provide these kinds of answers. It was clear that you had to look elsewhere to discover what really makes brands tick and if these tools did not produce the answer, then there had to be a different road that would lead to the essence of the brand. This set off the search for a solution that was to turn up some surprising discoveries. This is the story of how I followed this brand dream and brought it within every company's reach.

The timeline for the journey starts in the early 1990s and involved a number of client projects with prototypes of the still-evolving brand dream model. The first full brand dream programme that involved the application of the finished model was run for Bisto in 1996 shortly after I had formed The Gathering, a brand and innovation consultancy. A number of people, particularly Darrel Poulos, Giles Lenton and Heather Campbell, contributed to the thinking that went into the development of the process and model over the next few years. A number of Gathering colleagues, notably Marc Cox who joined me in 1997, were involved in running projects as part of the team and helped me to refine the way the brand dream programme was delivered.

Unravelling the brand enigma

Back in the late 1980s I was working with major blue-chip FMCG and retail brands. It was then that the whole brand dilemma came to a head for me. I had been getting increasingly frustrated with the conventional way in which brand development was tackled. At one level, it all seemed perfectly reasonable. Take a rebranding brief, carry out insight studies to find out how the brand was perceived, relate this to the business strategy and brand values and then propose something smarter. The trouble was that this left-brain, highly analytical approach was ploddingly unproductive. It was invariably difficult to get creative teams to get their minds round the implications of all these important aspects of the brief. Even more than that, marketing people usually had a very narrow and superficial grasp of what we were trying to do. They found it hard to understand the deeper strategic issues, or what gave the brand its edge. Bringing creative solutions to bear in these confused circumstances was next to impossible. The first clue came with a box of chocolates.

At the time I was working on a project to rebrand a specialist chain of chocolate shops with a fresh image intended to move them away from a rather clichéd ribbons-and-bows look. Yet every redesign proposal kept coming up with what were little more than variations of the same old chocolate-box image. Not surprisingly, all the suggestions were rejected by the client.

But then, not for the first time on this journey, serendipity came to the rescue. The unseen hand guided me to a psychologist who worked at the University of Toronto. As a result of a series of conversations between us, I saw a way of approaching the whole task in a different way.

After I explained my frustrations about communicating a complicated brief to the creative team, the psychologist talked about his use of techniques for helping people get beneath the surface of things to expose deeper issues and meanings. The upshot was that he offered to spend a day helping us to think laterally about the values and motivation factors behind brands. Rather than approaching the redesign brief head on, he encouraged the team to loosen up, and use free association and other techniques to get at what lay behind the surface of the company and the products it sold.

Principle One: If you stay on the surface you will never understand what lies underneath

The experiment worked. Using this less rigidly analytical framework threw up fresh ideas about the nutrition and enjoyment factors around chocolate. Previously, the team had been stuck with the tired and obvious connection between chocolate and indulgence. This sparked off a new line of creative thought and the stores were reconceived as places that communicated food values, rather like a specialist delicatessen. The client liked this fresh approach and we went ahead with the redesign on themes that represented a break with the past chocolate-box clichés.

For the first time, I felt that I had found a means of helping a creative team to tease out the essence and spirit of a brand. This lateral approach was the first step in the evolution of what is now known as the brand dream concept. Following this rebranding exercise I felt that I was at last on to something promising: an alternative means of getting beneath the surface of brands and coming up with something different and compelling. While I had discovered a practical way of getting people to unlock hidden aspects of the brand, I was well aware that this was only part of the solution. There had to be additional, complementary ways of jump-starting the creative process. Once again, it was to be a client project that helped to pull the next part of the brand dream picture into focus.

When I returned from Canada to Europe, I began to apply what I had learnt to get closer to the energy sources that drive brands. By now, I was sure that the way forward lay in developing experiential events, collaborative activities and opportunities for pooling shared experience.

On one corporate project I found myself working alongside a team development specialist who specialised in outward-bound ventures. One afternoon over a cup of tea, he asked me what I was doing next week. I replied that I had my hands full completing three large office-based design assignments. When he told me that he was taking the board of directors from a Fortune 500 company trekking across the Appalachian Mountains that week as part of a team-building exercise, I realised that here was another method of getting people to make connections that were impossible in a day-to-day working environment. I asked myself, 'How could I bring some of this into my work?'

I had spent a lot of time working out the implications of harnessing the creativity of the team as a group and this had inspired me to bring a range of experiential activities into the process. The outward-bound option offered another way of jolting people into a new way of looking at things.

In parallel with the development of methods and techniques, I had been developing a framework for channelling the creative process. Other ways of dealing with the brand challenge were falling into place. By 1995, a prototype for the brand dream model had been conceived. The model represented three interlocking elements representing the traditions of the brand, the behaviour that informed the way in which the brand behaves and the over-riding dream or vision. I now had a model that I could present to people, which could be used to explore their own brands. Deceptively simple, but extremely powerful in its application, the brand dream model provided a way of focusing people's attention on the brand attributes that really mattered. There were still other key elements to be discovered, though.

Around this time, another project with one of the world's major cleaning products and furniture care companies took me to the next step in evolving the brand dream process.

Principle Two: Location, location, location – never underestimate the magical power of place to energise or demotivate the creative process

The project involved getting 25 people together for an innovation session. As we needed to fly people in for this project, the project manager said 'Why don't we go somewhere different?' We ended up going to St Paul de Vence in Southern France and booking in to a traditional back-street hotel nestling in the seventeenth-century cobbled streets.

As the group gathered at Heathrow, clearly the atmosphere in the departure lounge was electric. Everyone was energised by the thought of going somewhere different and inspiring. Nor were they disappointed in the results. The project was extremely successful in terms of breakthrough innovative thought, fun and team building. It was simply terrific.

This revealed another principle of the brand dream process. Taking people out of their humdrum workplace and putting them into a stimulating environment can spark a different order of energy and creativity. The experience made me realise that place and location could be crucial in shaping the mood and energy of the group. You can hold a meeting anywhere. But when you are trying to achieve something out of the ordinary, the surroundings play an enormously important part in stimulating or deadening people's response. There is plenty of evidence that creative thinking is most likely to take place in situations where people are freed up from routine and the preoccupations of everyday responsibilities. Getting away from it can be the best way to create the conditions for inspirational ideas to flower.

Principle Three: Use all your faculties, not just your intellect, to see things in new ways

The next milestone on the journey was meeting another extraordinary person. Heather Campbell brings something rather different to the table. She is an expert in shamanistic practices and has brought the insights gained from her knowledge of Native American culture to help businesses see change and other issues from a new perspective. She encouraged me to extend the search for alternative ways of exploring the spirit of an organisation and its brand. Having already concluded that a conventional left-brain approach was never going to generate breakthrough results, the world of shamanistic rituals and activities proved to be an important source of inspiration for what I was trying to do.

By now the whole perception issue had started to move centre stage for me. I was convinced that enabling people to see things in new and unaccustomed ways was crucial to their ability to come up with innovative solutions. While the first insight into the value of lateral thinking had come thanks to my Canadian psychologist, I was only part of the way down the road to creating experiential group activities that would help to move people out of the established tram lines of conventional thinking. Working with Heather helped me to add a whole new dimension to the brand dream process.

Spending time with her was an education in Native American philosophy and ritual which provided me with some valuable clues about how to solve this problem. Particularly eye opening were the concepts of male energy and female energy, the former associated with logic and analysis, the latter with reflective and meditative practices. There are parallels here with the Eastern concept of Yin and Yang, which similarly represents a union of opposite, but complementary forms of energy, like the positive and negative poles of a magnet. It was another way of looking at what I had already concluded was an imbalance in the way we favoured analytical over intuitive approaches to solving problems. The Native American tradition provided a framework to demonstrate the relationship between these faculties and the importance of maintaining a productive balance. There were also other useful insights from the way they describe our make-up and the way to realise our potential as human beings. More about that in the panel below.

Seeing the world the medicine wheel way

There are several ways of interpreting medicine wheels. They can be seen laid out in large stone circles with radiating rows or spokes of stones in many parts of the American continent, the oldest dating back 4500 years. According to Hopi tradition, the cardinal points of the circle are associated with the four elements and four aspects of human nature. North is associated with air, or mental faculties. South represents water and the emotions. West represents our physical nature and East is associated with fire and the spiritual aspect. Heather Campbell explains how this plays out in life.

'As human beings, we have four aspects or energies that shape our lives: the physical – how we move our bodies; the mental – how we create ideas, memories and belief systems; the emotional aspect – the flow and ebb of our feelings; and spiritual – our focus on the unseen forces that shape our destiny, our quest for meaning. These aspects constantly interact with each other and create the complex web which is our life. Disharmony and problems arise when we favor one or more energies above the others – when the aspects are out of balance.'[19]

---

[19] *Sacred Business*, David Firth and Heather Campbell, Capstone, 1997.

Each of these four dimensions has positive as well as negative traits. For example, positive mental attributes are open-mindedness and creative thinking while the negative side is seen in dogmatism and rigidity. Similarly, the dark side of emotions is manifested in bottled-up feelings or being out of control and the light side means a free-flowing expression of feelings. Those living with an inner fire and passion demonstrate the light side of their spiritual aspect as opposed to the dark side, a passionless existence or adopting the visions of other people. Finally, those who have an openness to change and whose actions are consistent with what they say are in the positive zone of the physical aspect compared with those who over-emphasise the macho, aggressive side of their nature.

What Heather Campbell had observed from her work as a consultant helping companies to manage change was that there was over-reliance on logic, analysis and male energies. While this is essential for driving projects, it is not the way to win support or encourage inclusiveness. Yet companies often neglected the complementary role of female energies in turning goals into action. 'It also denies the receptive creativity, the hunches and intuitions and the powers of image and symbol which are associated with feminine energy.'[20]

All this helped to push my thinking along in what I could now see was a different but highly productive direction.

---

[20] *Sacred Business*, David Firth and Heather Campbell, Capstone, 1997.

This framework made explicit many of the ideas with which I was preoccupied around this time. It provided a coherent framework for thoughts that had been floating around in my head. This whole approach also made sense of what I had independently found to be wrong with the way in which people pursued solutions to problems, particularly when this called for real creativity.

I was also later struck by the similarities between Native American and Eastern philosophies and the way they emphasised the need for achieving balance between complementary energies, as well as the role of intuition in arriving at insights. The brand dream approach drew on all these systems of knowledge to develop what was missing from conventional approaches to problem-solving and creative projects.

I spent a lot of time researching Native American and Eastern traditions and exploring how to adapt the principles I discovered into the programme of activities I was developing. My goal was to help people break out of their usual patterns of thought and slip into more intuitive, imaginative and creative ways of seeing the world.

There are many reasons why I found Native American traditions a source of useful ideas. For one thing, because they were more attuned to intuitive ways of gaining knowledge, including their use of trance-inducing dances and music to achieve different states of consciousness. Another fascinating ritual that played an important part in a young brave's initiation into adult life was a medicine (meaning wisdom for Native Americans) journey. In their world, this lasted several weeks and involved spending a period of time living alone in the wild and fasting to induce inspirational visions. When a brave returned, his account of what he had experienced and seen was regarded as a vital part of the ritual. The tribal shaman and elders helped him to interpret the symbolism of events and sights he recalled, along with the decoding of significant dreams and visions that he had experienced.

Obviously, it was not going to be possible to send representatives from international companies into the wilderness for several weeks, or get them to follow Native American traditions exactly as practised in their culture. So I focused on replicating the essence of these practices and the purpose they performed. Following some experimentation, I was able to adapt and synthesise the most significant elements into the brand dream process to help bring about the necessary shifts in perception that I wanted to achieve. For example, I developed my own version of the medicine journey, but cut down to an hour or so to become a medicine walk. In a similar way, people apply the same terms of reference used by Native Americans to become aware of signs in the natural world, work on their symbolism and weave their experiences into a story that brings to life insights and ideas that they would never have uncovered through more Western-style debate or analysis. On the back of that I developed a way of collecting and synthesising all the individual strands to create a collective group story. The end result was a rich, experiential way for people to explore issues and share their insights collaboratively. More than that, it was an inclusive process in which everyone in the group participated and contributed to the corporate vision.

While people find this novel approach stimulating, even invigorating, what helps to make the exercise productive in brand dream terms is that the medicine walk has a focus. Before people set out they are invited to introduce a particular thought into their minds during their journey. The practical value from this exercise comes from the way their stories are interpreted. Over time, I became better able to form a sense of what these stories represented in the context of the brand dream process. It became easier to avoid the platitudes and go beyond the obvious to tease out insights of real significance.

One of the things that drew me to these traditions is that they are essentially right brain in nature, associated with intuition and imagination. The whole approach is a valuable counter-balance to the predominant Western emphasis on analytical and intellectual approaches to problem-solving. Interestingly, Native Americans passed on their knowledge by word of mouth. There was no written language. Instead of reading and writing about the world, they went out and lived existence through their other senses. Native Americans were orientated towards other modes of understanding, learning and seeing. Getting in touch with their way was to prove enormously valuable in enabling me to work with people to generate inspirational solutions.

Much of what we are learning from the science of the brain validates the basis for these modes of sensing and knowing the world.

The story of Jill Bolte Taylor, a Harvard-trained brain scientist, brings science and experience together through a twist of fate that enabled her to witness the impact that a left-hemisphere stroke had on the functioning of her own brain. Her extraordinary story has helped her to humanise the science of brain function in a way that transcends the matter-of-fact description you would expect from a scientific journal.

It started with a burst blood vessel in the left hemisphere of Taylor's brain. She remained sufficiently aware to observe with a neuroanatomist's acuity the progress of her disintegrating brain function. The first thing that registered was the loss of all the skills associated with analysis, normal cognition, as well as her ability to speak or understand others. At the same time, there was a sudden euphoric epiphany as the right brain took over and she became overwhelmed with a sensation of deep peace, oneness with existence and total immersion in the moment.

Over time, she recovered all her faculties and now uses her academic knowledge and personal experience to help others rebuild their lives after suffering strokes. But just as important to her was the revelation that the right brain could open the door to a new view of life and the world around us. The whole episode led her to become a passionate advocate for the power of our right-brain faculties to enable us to see things in a richer, more integrated way similar to that which ancient traditions had described and hinted at over the centuries.

She described the complementary roles of the brain to an audience of Technology, Entertainment and Design conference delegates.[21] Using a computing analogy, she likened the right hemisphere to a parallel processor and the left to a serial processor to sum up the fact that they operate in completely different ways. Although connected, they are completely separate.

'The right hemisphere thinks in pictures, and learns kinaesthetically through the movement of our bodies. Information in the form of energy streams in simultaneously through all our sensory systems and explodes into this enormous collage of what this present moment looks like, what this present

---

[21] Jill Bolte Taylor "Powerful Stroke of Insight", www.ted.com/themes/view/id/4

moment smells like and tastes like, what it feels like and what it sounds like.

Our left hemisphere thinks linearly and methodically. Our left hemisphere is all about the past and all about the future. Our left hemisphere is designed to take the enormous collage of the present moment and start picking out details and more details, and details about those details ... it categorises and organises all that information and associates it with every-thing in the past we've ever learned and projects into the future all our possibilities. Our left hemisphere thinks in language ...'

While not completely in accord on all the details, science seems to agree with the fundamental insights of ancient tra-ditions that human capabilities span an impressive spectrum. Whatever the language that is used to describe this spectrum, the practical message is that acknowledging the full range of analytical to intuitive faculties is a first step to making better use of our whole minds.

Principle Four: Conventional methods produce conventional results. Trust your intuition to lead you where you need to go

Despite all the evidence underpinning Principle Four, the fact remains that business is predominantly more comfortable with logical, analytical processes. Also, all this may sound wacky and off the wall to anyone who has no first-hand experience of these traditions and alternative methods of looking at the world. Nonetheless, virtually everyone involved in brand dream projects over the years, from chief executives and cynical sales managers to creatives and clerical staff, has been prepared to put their reservations to one side and give the benefit of doubt to what they may initially regard as weird ways of running a project. Almost without exception, the most common reaction is one of pleasant surprise. Even more important, the results from scores of client projects confirm that the approach used in the brand dream process really does get to parts of the corporate psyche that conventional techniques never reach. The output from these sessions has variously been new ideas, new campaigns and brand development plans that have led to higher performance.

By the late 1990s I had come a long way from initial dissatisfaction with traditional approaches to brand development and marketing. The brand dream concept was more or less complete by this stage, and from then on it was a matter of turning up the volume and adding other variations on the same theme of right-brain creativity. It was not only other philosophies and traditions that showed how to achieve the perception shifts we needed to make. In the same way that I had taken a cue from Native American culture, I also borrowed from Eastern philosophies, as well as from the worlds of music, theatre, poetry and other art forms to find ways of breaking through the concrete of conventional thought to ignite the creative spark.

For example, it is surprising how effective putting together a short dramatic sketch can be to cut through to what people really see as the core issues that concern them most. Or how a simple drawing exercise can open the door that enables people to see connections that were invisible to them before. Everyone is able to express themselves to an adequate level in all these different media. And although many people will never have tried their hand at these activities since school, they sometimes amaze themselves with their efforts in a non-competitive, collaborative environment. Rather like the medicine walk and other right-brain methods we use, the whole point is to trigger associations and ideas that are not readily accessible through analysis and debate. Another important point is that all of the activities that have been incorporated into the brand dream process are group-based.

Over the years, we have used group involvement techniques including drumming, singing, dance, theatre, art, storytelling, meditation and even martial arts, and we are constantly refreshing the ways in which we stimulate creativity and collaboration. Apart from anything else, all of these activities have the value of getting people to collaborate in ways that are novel and that they would not normally employ at work. This means that they also see aspects of each other's personalities and talents that are rarely apparent in the workplace. Another plus-point that became apparent in the early experiments with different techniques for stimulating creativity: they were all energising. Rather than leaving people punch-drunk from endless presentations, or dry debates, the brand dream process invariably left people on a high. Not least, these activities are absorbing and fun.

Principle Five: If you are not enjoying yourself and thinking intuitively, then you are not going to be creative

The stimulating, fun aspect of the brand dream process has been a source of amazement for more than one client. During what was to be a milestone event in the evolution of the brand dream process, 20 people from one of the world's leading food companies had gathered together at a venue in the Cotswolds. In the afternoon of the first day, two of the project managers came up to me and asked what drugs we'd put in the lunch. They had never been on a project where everyone had been so enthused and outgoing before.

One of the ways we did this was by making sure that they were constantly involved in the process in a variety of different ways. Some exercises emphasised male energies, through drumming or other physical activities. Others involved more reflective tasks, like painting or music, drawing on female energies. Both types of exercise are means of helping them to enjoy the intuitive process. It was enormously powerful in its effect. As a result of the project the food company came up with business-changing concepts, which were to lead to a number of extremely successful product development initiatives.

The project experience showed how powerful connecting with the values behind the brand could be in bonding the marketing team and external agencies together. Later, when we went to see the team back in their office, the atmosphere was electric. They were proud to be part of this group brand feeling. They realised that over two days, they had revealed the secret life of the brand and made it explicit in a way that was there for all to see. That turned them on massively.

The outcome of this was to be a tremendous uplift in performance. It led to a regeneration of the brand, repositioning and a massive improvement in sales. The company became a marketing design effectiveness awards finalist and jumped 20 points up the supermarket brand league. Whole new areas were opened up for the business as a result of undergoing the brand dream process.

Principle Six: Once you change the way you feel about the whole brand experience, you can change the way the brand behaves

This was a Eureka moment. Although we had been using the brand dream model on assignments regularly, by the end of this project it became obvious that we had raised the process to a new level. The results showed that the experiential activities were having a profound effect, initially on the people involved in the project and then in influencing the behaviour of the brand itself as those involved on the two away days communicated their insights and enthusiasm to others back in the business.

Up to this point, the brand dream model had been proving its worth in a range of projects. But now, we had a more fully articulated process whose full value was apparent to our clients. It added up to a proven, tested and hugely inspiring way of working. And it was highly time-efficient. In most cases, it called for no more than a two-day programme of activities. And, if there were advertising and communications creatives involved, they would often have written the next commercial or script by the time they got back to the airport.

What we had discovered through the projects we had run was that they effectively became portals through which people could discover aspects of their brands that had either been overlooked, forgotten or simply never fully realised. We had also validated one of the core assumptions underpinning the brand dream process, namely that reawakening people's intuitive response was essential to shifting them to a frame of mind where they became aware of what really made the brand tick. By changing perceptions we were able to change behaviour and kick start a new cycle of creativity that translated into business results.

There have been many examples where, in Tom Peters' phrase, people have suddenly 'got it'. On one occasion, the creative team from an ad agency had been criticised by the client for being dull and uninspiring. They confessed that they were blocked about what to do. What's more, they were at war with the planners. But after they went through the programme they were a changed crew. Freshly inspired and motivated, they quickly came up with a solution that met with the client's approval.

The personal dividend

During and after the medicine walk there have been some extraordinary personal experiences.

Sometimes people have ended up in physical and mental places they never expected. Like the merchandise planner who went on a medicine walk and did not come back for three hours, looking rather sheepish for being away so long but enlightened about the problem he was trying to solve. Only later did we learn that he had climbed a tree and become so absorbed in his train of thought that he lost all track of time.

In Milan, a senior sales executive came back in tears. He had wandered into the Duomo, which sparked an inspirational, spiritual experience.

On another occasion, a brand dream event was planned at a remote resort between Sweden and Norway. Several people sensed a bad atmosphere about the place. Someone complained of a blackness and heaviness. When we looked into the history of the location, we discovered a grim history that fully justified this sombre image of the place.

The significance of these examples? They are evidence that once people give themselves a chance, they can tune in to other modes of looking at things and sensing the world around them. Everyone can switch into an intuitive approach to problems – including brand issues they are trying to resolve. The process gives them permission to operate in a way that is refreshingly different from the workaday life. One participant summed up the reaction of many when he said: 'You know, I can't remember the last time I was given an opportunity to reflect on anything at work.'

This was the trail that led to the evolution of the brand dream model, something which continues to evolve as new projects bring fresh insights on how to improve the process.

Stories with a point

One of the sub-themes running through this book is the need to redress the imbalance that has led us to put so much of our trust in our analytical powers at the expense of other instinctive, emotional and spiritual faculties that make us what we are. The Native Americans, like many other ancient traditions, did not suffer from this lopsided view of human nature. Their view was integrated and holistic. Rediscovering this fount of knowledge and what it had to offer was an important step on the journey.

There is also plenty of new thinking about innovation, creativity and fostering change that takes account of people as human beings, rather than factors of production. There is fresh evidence that shows taking a whole-person approach to finding solutions really does pay off.

You need look no further than the work of Steve Denning, the architect of a new approach to leading change. It may be novel in a corporate context, but storytelling is as ancient as speech itself. He discovered that used in the right way, stories can strike a chord in ways that PowerPoint presentations can never achieve.

Formerly programme director, knowledge management at the World Bank, Steve Denning was bemused by reliance on fact-dense arguments to win people round to change despite the evidence of the failure of these one-way communications blitzes to have the intended effect. He started exploring the power of what he was later to call 'springboard' stories as a means of engaging people so that they not only got the point, but also became co-conspirators in the plan. But this is not storytelling for storytelling's sake. There is a clear, pragmatic agenda. The story is a means to an end, rather than the kind of bravura performance that you expect from a best-selling novelist. Instead, it involves a minimalist approach that leaves plenty of room for the listener to fill in the blanks so it then becomes their story as well. 'In contrast to logic and analysis, storytelling shyly invites collaboration, and in so doing, gains privileged access to the back door of the mind.'[22]

This is what I was after: finding ways of getting people to become engaged on their own terms in the whole process of discovering the spirit of the brand. It is no use simply telling people what you want them to hear. You have to find ways of getting them to become part of the conspiracy. Any method that gains access to the back door of the mind offers a better way of engaging people than bombarding them with facts and slogans.

[22] *The Springboard*, Stephen Denning, Butterworth Heinemann, 2001.

FITTING THE
PIECES
TOGETHER

THE
BRAND DREAM MODEL

CHAPTER 5

'Time present and time past
Are both perhaps present in time future
And time future contained in time past.'

T. S. Eliot, Burnt Norton, Four Quartets

As the story of the evolution of the brand dream described in the previous chapter explained, it was a journey born of frustration with the whole way in which companies have traditionally managed their brands. This mounting dissatisfaction led to a search for other methods of stimulating creative solutions and escaping from largely unproductive and tired approaches to brand management. In many ways the mission was extremely ambitious. We set out to solve not only one set of process-related problems. We also wanted to provide a tool kit that companies could use to deconstruct their brands and reassemble them based on a whole set of fresh insights into what they were all about. Having decoded the brand, the pieces of the puzzle needed to be reconstructed in a form that could be understood and applied throughout the business.

Just as we felt that the answer to the process challenge was not going to be found in the standard brand development manual, so we took a first-principles approach to creating the brand dream model. It had to have the virtues of being highly practical, capable of inspiring action and being memorable. So in parallel with the exploration of experiential processes and methods for posing questions about the brand, we started to build a simple yet powerful framework that could be used to make the brand dream visible. But that was still only part of our mission.

Any model had to do much more than simply record the output of the processes. We wanted something that could be readily understood and relevant to the whole organisation, not just the marketing professionals. This was another reason why the choice of words used to capture the dream was crucial. Any slogan had to be as crisp as the snappiest advertising slogan, but with a depth that made the brand's aspirations crystal clear to everyone.

In the future, the brand dream model was intended to provide a reference point and a guide for a wide range of purposes: new product development, innovation, brand extensions, packaging, design, logos and promotional materials, in fact any activity where it was essential that the genius of the brand was reflected. The model was also intended to be a touchstone for adjusting and refining business strategy in line with the brand dream. Losing sight of that dream, or failing to rejuvenate it at critical points in the life cycle of the business, could have disastrous consequences – as we will see in Chapter Seven. Equally, when the brand dream loses its focus or is somehow diluted, the business can easily drift or lose momentum.

Our experience suggested that an effective brand dream could be the life force of an enterprise because it touched all aspects of organisational life and culture and could be used to drive staff motivation and engagement and influence the quality of their relationships with fellow workers, customers and business partners. This is why we attached so much importance to discovering and harnessing the energy of the brand dream for the whole organisation. That job becomes trickier when the chief dreamer who originally created the business is no longer in place to ensure that the brand and everyone who works under its banner remains aligned with that formative vision.

So we stripped down the model to what we saw as the essential DNA of the brand, the genetic features that made it great in the first place and defined the opportunities for taking it to the next phase of growth. This is the model in its simplest outline form:

- Traditions – the living, enduring legacy of the brand.
- Behaviour – the values that shape the behaviour of the brand.

- Dream – the inspirational vision that directs the evolution of the brand.

These elements of the brand also provide three windows over time: past (the traditions); present (behaviour); and

THE BRAND DREAM MODEL

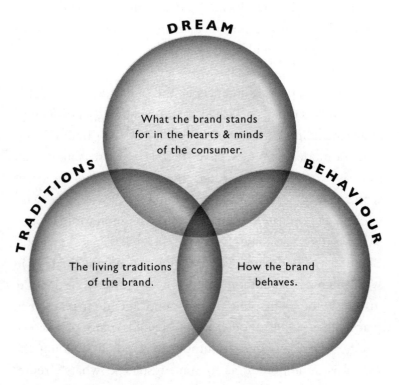

DREAM

What the brand stands for in the hearts & minds of the consumer.

TRADITIONS

BEHAVIOUR

The living traditions of the brand.

How the brand behaves.

The three circles of the brand dream model

future (dream). Combined, they represent the distinctive genius of the brand.

Changing operating conditions, new threats and opportunities, as well as the emerging organisation and culture of the business, mean that the brand dream needs to be regularly recalibrated to keep pace with new developments in the marketplace as well as the company's changing circumstances. Maintaining that dynamic balance over time is crucial, and the interlocking circles are a reminder that constantly balancing this relationship is the smart way to ensure continuity and solid growth.

Like so many powerful concepts, the brand dream model is deceptively simple. In design, it is uncluttered and deliberately streamlined, in contrast with a lot of other brand development models you may have seen. For that reason, it is all too easy to underestimate the importance of the choice of words that fit each circle. For example, it would be easy enough to populate the three circles with more-or-less plausible words to describe the dream, behaviour and traditions. But the brand dream model is not a cerebral exercise in wordsmithing. Its authority and power derive from the way in which the right phrases are found and then planted in place. Process and model are inseparable parts of a single whole. The experiential journey involved in building the model is as important as the end result. So what is represented in the finally agreed, carefully crafted model is the visible summary of a much deeper and more expansive brand reality.

There is a time and place in the brand dream process for reflecting on the insights that are generated in the course of the journey and agreeing the final choice of words that capture the spirit of the brand, but that is at the end, not the start. But the real work involves right-brain creativity rather than relying on the analytical, brainstorming approach to discovering answers that many brand development methods depend on. The whole aim is to coax people into a mental space where they stop juggling with words and start tapping into their intuition, feelings and emotional faculties. The experiential approach holds the key to understanding what has been, is now and could be in the future.

If this sounds hard to envisage, remember the way in which Dickens' *Christmas Carol* made the transformational power of experience the heart of his story of the redemption of Ebenezer Scrooge from heartless miser to decent human being. Demonstrating a sound grasp of practical psychology, the ghosts of Christmas Past and Future decided that lecturing Scrooge on his shortcomings was never going to do the trick. Instead, they transported the penny-pinching grouch through time to revisit his past and then taste the miserable fate awaiting him, assuming he did nothing to mend his ways. It is only a story, of course, but nonetheless a compelling example that shows how experience can be a powerful persuader. Although the context may be somewhat different, a similar principle is embedded in the brand dream process which takes people on a similar journey into past and future. The aim is comparable: to help individuals connect with their brand traditions and envision future possibilities in ways that connect with what matters personally to them rather than through chalk-and-talk presentations that cast them in the role of passive consumers of information.

The previous chapter described in some detail how we discovered and adapted the experiential techniques that became the building blocks used for this purpose. Broadly, they fall into two main groups that fulfil different roles at various stages of the brand time-travel journey and are described in more detail in Chapter Four. The first set of exercises involves physical, pulse-raising activities that put people in a highly alert frame of mind. These are at the male-energy end of the spectrum. The second group of activities, associated with female energy, are reflective, meditative and intuitive in nature. These are intended to bubble up insights, new thoughts and ideas. Using this range of exercises, group members become time travellers and explore the three circles of the model. What is special about the whole programme is that it is shared and, not least, certain to be the kind of event that people are unlikely to forget in a hurry.

An inclusive process for everyone from CEO to floor sweeper

Now for how all this is put together. In structure, the brand dream process is more like an event than a meeting. The beauty of the brand dream model and accompanying process is that they are inclusive. They do not depend on specialist knowledge and skills of the kind that would be familiar to brand or marketing professionals. In many cases, it is all the more effective when a brand dream project involves a wide cross-section of staff, from the CEO to the floor sweeper, for the good reason that as a living entity the brand is shaped by the working practices and behaviour of everyone who works in the company and manifests itself in corporate culture and the way the organisation operates. It is not a construct of marketing's exclusive making.

The brand dream approach draws on the collective experience and knowledge of the group. Particularly in drawing on the group's collective memory, the process benefits from references to stories and traditions that illuminate the traditions of the brand. At each stage of the journey all the participants contribute their experiences, thoughts and ideas to create first a spectrum of opinion that is refined down to produce a view that captures the essence of the brand's living traditions.

In broad outline, the brand dream model moves through three phases. In the discovery phase, we set out to find how people inside the organisation view the current status of the organisation, including their views about strategy, the highs and lows, triumphs and disasters, what it is like to work inside the organisation, its reputation and standing, and the sense of brand identity. Normally this involves people who represent every strata of the enterprise.

Next, the brand dream event is organised to generate the brand dream model. This could involve 30 or more people selected for their responsibilities or representation of key groups within the organisation.

Following that, the core group reconvenes to review and if necessary refine the agreed wording of the brand dream model.

Enrolment entails putting as many people as possible from the organisation through a brand dream event to immerse them in the agreed brand dream model.

Finally, we go back to evaluate the impact that the adoption of the brand dream model has had on the performance of the organisation.

The core of the whole programme is the brand dream event.

Raising the curtain on the brand dream event

To ensure that everyone has their bearings throughout the whole process, there is a brief teach-in on the brand dream model, the philosophy behind it and the way it is used. Right at the outset, we take great pains to define for project participants exactly what we mean by the terms 'brand', 'dream', 'traditions' and 'behaviour' in this context. To make the concept come alive, we provide a few examples of how the brand dream model can be applied to leading brands. This also acts as a prelude to their first task. We start as we intend to go on by involving people in an exercise that enables them to get a feel for what they will be doing later on.

Once we have filled a flip chart with examples of well-known brands, they break into small groups and set about creating a rough-and-ready brand dream model, completing each of the three circles with an appropriate phrase based on their knowledge of the brand. There is always someone from the team to give them a nudge in the right direction if they get stuck. Having created this trial model, each team has the chance to talk through its choice of phrases and how this sums up the brand. That primes the pump for the real work ahead. This is more of an orientation exercise to make people comfortable with what the brand dream model is all about and what they will be setting out to achieve in relation to their own brand.

At this stage, they might have the broad idea of what is involved. But they will have no idea of what will be involved in coming up with the answers for their brand dream model. Over the course of two days, the typical duration for a brand dream programme, participants are engaged in a series of exercises that demand their full attention. One thing we can be certain about is that there is little chance of anyone getting bored. Some individuals may find they are amazed at what they learn about themselves as well as the brand. Some may find aspects of the programme unusual, even challenging. No one falls asleep at the back.

Rediscovering the legacy and traditions of the brand

Traditions. This circle relates to the key events and ideas associated with the origins of the brand, including the original vision, performance and values that contributed to its success in its formative days. The objective here is not just to revisit what made it great at the outset but to identify the living traditions of the brand, what has been carried forward to the present day and what, if anything, has been lost or modified over time. There is a story to be told that people need to understand. As marketing maestro and maverick Seth Godin points out in his blog, we are wired for stories. 'Stories define everything you say and do. The product has a myth, the service has a legend. Marketing applies to every person, every job, every service and every organisation. That's because all we can work with as humans is stories.'[23]

To get everyone into an active, collaborative mood, we ask them to take part in an energy-raising exercise. This proves to people that even if they have never tried something previously, they can learn to put together an impressive synchronised performance in very short order. It gets people talking, feeling quietly pleased with what they can do and ready for more interactive work.

Starting with a blank sheet of paper, the group then digs into their collective memories about the brand's history. This is a facilitated process that draws out a list of attributes that depicts a mosaic of influences, aspirations, triumphs and disappointments in the brand's past. Inevitably, longer-serving members of the company will have a fuller knowledge of the brand's past and this journey down memory lane can present a golden opportunity for newcomers to the organisation to learn about the origins and development of the brand from older hands.

The play's the thing

You can talk about the past. Or you can bring it to life dramatically. Sketches are one of a number of experiential group

---

[23] http://sethgodin.typepad.com/seths_blog/2008/06/index.html

activities that may be used to get to the heart of the issues around the past.

What comes out of a piece of drama is often more revealing and spontaneous than any dispassionate discussion about the bare facts. You will remember that Shakespeare used this device in *Hamlet* when the prince creates a play, with the help of a troupe of travelling players, to re-enact the poisoning of his father, the former king, by his mother's lover and current consort: 'The play's the thing to catch the conscience of the king,' reckons Hamlet, who is duly rewarded by the involuntary reflex Hamlet hopes for by tweaking the guilty conscience of the murderer who stole his father's position.

While the stakes may not be as high as in Hamlet's case, the use of theatre to portray aspects of the brand's legacy is a remarkably powerful way of actualising and communicating what people really feel. Taking the output from the earlier exploration of the brand's legacy and traditions, each team devises a short sketch that brings their observations to life for them. It is entirely up to them how they do this. It may be through a comic sketch or adapting historical, dramatic or mythical characters and events – it is invariably amazing what a group of people can conjure up with no more than 15 minutes' preparation. Depending on the overall size of the group, there can be several mini-productions that bring the history to life.

The extraordinary thing about this exercise is that it reveals, often with far more candour and transparency than any statement of fact can achieve, how people see the brand. These impromptu performances are inclusive and unfailingly informative, and invariably entertaining. Some reveal a touch of genius, although they are not, of course, intended to seek out budding Mike Leighs. Even those who are not natural performers are prepared to become involved. The 'You-won't-catch-me-doing-that' response is rarely encountered. Most throw themselves willingly into the theatrical exercise and find themselves carried along with the spirit of the moment.

By the conclusion of this phase of the project, people have gained insights into the brand's legacy that may well have been unfamiliar or half forgotten. Most importantly, though, the whole group has a shared understanding of the most significant formative influences in the development of the brand, along with the twists and turns in its evolution. All this is decanted into a summary of the key features and influences, both positive and negative, on the brand's development and most importantly what they mean for the brand in its present incarnation.

Brand behaviour and the personal connection

Behaviour. This is all about how the brand is actualised through corporate culture and people's behaviour. The focus is on the present: what the brand means to people in their daily working lives and how it influences their dealings with colleagues, partners, other stakeholders and not least customers. Above all, the goal is to describe not just the current reality, but how people would ideally like their brand to behave and the values they believe should shine through.

Overall, the outcome from this phase is to set the standard for attitudes and behaviour across the organisation: what should the members of the organisation, the ambassadors of the brand, understand to be its core values and how, as a result, should they behave? The brand dream objective is to help everyone establish connections between their passions and enthusiasms and things that are important to them as individuals and brand values. Or put another way, this part of the programme sets out to identify the crossover between personal and corporate life.

Again, just as with other phases of the programme, rather than asking everyone just to talk about the issues, these associations are surfaced through a number of appropriate exercises. In this case the emphasis is more on reflective activities, including some form of art-related self-expression to represent personal values symbolically.

Once again, people are asked to do something that is outside their normal everyday experience. This can involve drawing, and even those who may never have done this since their school days can find it a quietly satisfying experience.

At the conclusion of the exercise individuals are brought back to reflect on the significance of what they have created and its relevance to the organisation's brand values. Even when there is no obvious vocational connection with their jobs, people are almost always able to find a bridge that links their personal enthusiasms to organisational and brand values.

At the end of this session, the key attributes that sum up the brand's behaviour are distilled from the output of these individual explorations of personal and corporate values and behavioural traits. This marks the completion of the second phase of the brand dream process and sets the stage for the final leg of the journey.

Phase Four: The dream and the guiding principle for brand development

Dream. This is not simply a restatement of the original dream which inspired the creation of the business, but a fresh definition of the overarching vision that will shape the future from this point on. The aim is to summarise what the group wants the brand to be known for in the hearts and minds of customers and other stakeholders.

When we talk about a 'dream' in this context it is important to be clear about what is meant. It is not the same thing as a mission statement, which is about the achievement of a specific business goal. A classic example of a well-defined mission statement is contained in President John Kennedy's 1961 Congress address, when he stated his 'goal, before this decade is out, of landing a man on the Moon and returning him safely to the Earth.'[24] It was time-bounded, 'before this decade is out'; concrete, 'landing a man on the moon'; and complete, 'returning him safely to the Earth'.

By contrast, a dream is bigger and more aspirational. For example, in the Kennedy speech, the dream was to help secure 'our future on earth' by playing 'a leading role in space achievement'. In other words, a dream is the encapsulation of a stretching, highly ambitious, but not unattainable vision of possibilities that is compelling enough to capture the imagination of those who work for the organisation. The dream should be inspirational. The mission tells the organisation what needs to be done to make it come true.

Dreams sustain successful businesses. Apple's ambition to create 'insanely great computers' lies behind its record for continuing to wow its fans with innovations in design, from the first Macintosh cube computer through to the iMac and

---

[24] President John F. Kennedy's 'Man on the Moon' Address to Congress, 25th May 1961.

its latest Air computer. Nike's 'Irreverence justified' sums up its commitment to constantly support athletes' pursuit of improved performance, not only in the quality of its sports equipment but by fighting their cause. It is no accident that these companies have acquired legendary status as super brands. Everything they do is aligned behind a single-minded sense of direction. The challenge for the brand dream group is to rekindle the dream that will fire their own organisation's ambition to succeed.

By this stage, people will have travelled backwards in time to familiarise themselves with the original inspiration for the business and revisited the evolution of the brand and its ups and downs over the years. Although understanding the history of the brand provides the foundation for building a solid future, many other brand development programmes miss out this step in the dash for solutions. Brand dream project managers confirm that assimilating the implications of a brand's history and evolution over time is crucial to making well-informed choices about its future. The review of the past provides an opportunity to build on strengths and de-emphasise aspects of the brand that are either negative or no longer relevant.

Arriving at that redefinition of the dream can be a tough call and is something that demands a little inspiration in its own right. The medicine walk, a modified version of the Native American quest for enlightenment, gives people an opportunity to gain a different perspective on what should be at the heart of their ambition. What had become clear from applying this modified approach to unlocking intuitive thoughts was that it could enable people to look at everything in a new way. It takes people beyond their normal thinking habits into a zone where out-of-the-ordinary patterns and associations can lead to genuinely fresh insights.

First, people are put into the right frame of mind where they are more likely to make these intuitive connections. A visualisation exercise provides a quick route to take people away from the buzz of the everyday world into a calmer, more reflective state. Next comes the walk. Everyone follows their own individual route and observes whatever sights and events impress themselves on their mind. At some stage in their walk, when they feel the time is right, they allow a simple, predefined question about their vision for the brand to enter their minds and register any thoughts that formulate themselves by way of response. As well as bringing back any answers that they discover as a result, they are also asked to bring back any natural or man-made objects from their medicine walk that represent a token of an insight or significant event they have witnessed.

After they return – usually after about an hour or so – they gather together and each in turn relates the story of their journey, bringing out the thoughts and impressions that are sparked by what they have seen and encountered. These sessions are facilitated by members of the brand dream team to tease out the significance and relevance to the objective for this final session. The way in which these thoughts and ideas are harvested, first from individuals, then their immediate groups and finally through a plenary gathering of everyone who participated in the programme, underlines the inclusive and consensual nature of the whole brand dream process. At the end of the two days, the group will have developed a fresh version of the dream to which everyone has contributed and to which everyone feels they can subscribe.

The final act is to formulate a single brand dream model for the organisation that summarises the important living traditions of the brand, its most significant values and behavioural characteristics, or the brand behaviour, and the dream, or overarching, inspiring vision for the future development of the brand and the enterprise.

A process that embeds the brand in the organisational psyche

There is little doubt that the brand dream process is a far cry from the typical development project with which most companies will be familiar. Compared with the formal way in which meetings, discussions and projects are organised, there is a touch of unconventional and unexpected non-conformity about the whole process. But the output is the real test of its validity. As the feedback from companies confirms in the next chapter, those that have deployed the brand dream process have achieved results that are highly rewarding, with unexpected bonuses into the bargain. 'High risk, high reward' were the words used by one project sponsor. A lot of this is down to how people react to novel ways of problem-solving that are radically different from the custom-and-practice techniques used in business. For most people, the experiential nature of the process is a breath of fresh air.

Experiences speak louder than words. That is really what the brand dream process is about: an absorbing experience that taps into right-brain capabilities and faculties that modern life has done its best to relegate to secondary status. At one level, the brand dream model is a celebration of our creative and innovative capabilities, directed towards the goal of discovering the soul of the organisation. But, as the experience of companies that have deployed the programme reports, putting the whole brain to work really does take some beating when you are looking for sparkling results.

Taking the
Brand Dream Medicine

'He who is not courageous enough to take risks will accomplish nothing in life.'

Muhammad Ali

Creating the brand dream process and model is one thing. But how does it play out in practice for those who have applied it to their organisation's brands? This chapter looks at the experience of a number of people who have made the journey as brand dream sponsors. It looks at what they wanted to achieve, and their reflections on the experience of the whole programme, both for them personally and their teams. It also gives an account of the outcome of their projects.

They provide the ultimate test of the brand dream process. How far will it help these different organisations to refresh their understanding of their brands? Does the experiential approach work in public as well as commercial organisations? What about the ability of the process to embed an understanding of the brand across the team? Or to come up with genuine insights that set the enterprise on a new growth track?

Over the years the brand dream process has been applied to a wide range of organisations, including various types of consumer and industrial businesses, a school and a government department. What unites all these different kinds of organisations is a need to gain a better understanding of what was different and special about their operations and how insights into the spirit of their brand could help them to improve their performance.

The following examples reflect the experience of a selection of these brand dreamers over six different projects in different organisational contexts and differing brand circumstances.

These individual stories reveal a number of common themes.

First, in several cases the brand dream approach succeeded in bringing about results of a kind and within a timeframe that would have been impossible in other ways. Also, in several cases, programme sponsors achieved benefits over and above those that they had anticipated or expected.

Second, the experiential dimension of the process proved to be a valuable differentiating factor and a big plus when the brand dream model is compared with alternative development methods and techniques. In virtually every case, the journey involved in reaching a consensus around brand values turned out to be as important as the redefined brand dream and values in establishing a sense of common purpose.

Third, a valuable byproduct of the process was team building. The inclusive nature of the experiential exercises pulled people together around a shared view of the brand that made them feel part of the defining process.

Fourth, the power and simplicity of the model proved to be hugely valuable for communicating the brand dream, for the benefit of both internal and external marketing professionals working on brand development, as well as other members from the top to the bottom of the organisation.

Fifth, despite an initial scepticism about the unorthodox nature of the approach, sponsors found that it achieved their goals, despite the apprehension of some of the participants.

Sixth, the process provided an opportunity for people to experience the brand as a living entity rather than as a dry, intellectual concept.

In summary, there were big pay-offs and benefits, most notably:

- The formulation of a redefined brand dream.
- A shared understanding of brand values within and beyond the marketing function.

- A clear set of principles for guiding brand development and marketing initiatives.
- A powerful tool for directing innovation and brand strategy.

The fact remains, though, that sponsors of the brand dream model recognised that they were dealing with what Nick Shepherd, formerly with Kraft, defined as a 'High risk, high reward' project.

On the one hand, programme leaders recognised that there was the possibility of breakthrough improvements. On the other hand, they were keenly aware that this meant moving people out of their comfort zone. The calculation they had to make was simple. Keep doing the same old things in the same old way, and do not expect to achieve anything but the same old results. Or, try something radically different, with the prospect of making a significant leap forward. In these particular instances, brand dream sponsors decided that there was far more to be won than lost in going for it.

It is always tempting with hindsight to airbrush out the difficult issues and leave a picture that looks too good to be true. Here, the programme sponsors speak frankly about their concerns as well as their expectations in the run up to their brand dream projects. Not least, they describe how their adventures with the brand dream process turned out, the impact on people and the ultimate value gained. The rewards more than justified the risks.

Polishing up a brand's diamond qualities

'I first met Duncan when he was working for an agency and we were working with them on the Carte Noire coffee brand because the original French solution didn't work for us. Duncan ended up as the project director and demonstrated his commercial abilities in repositioning the brand. It was a fantastic experience for us.'

Almost as a kind of precursor to a memorable and eventful brand dream exercise, the main meeting for this project was scheduled for 15.00 on a Christmas Eve at Swindon, between Kraft's Cheltenham offices and London where Duncan was based. A snowstorm whiteout made travel an endurance test. Against the odds, the rendezvous was kept, the meeting produced results and Nick Shepherd recalls that his parting shot to Duncan's team was to wish them 'Good luck. I hope you get home for Christmas.'

After that, the next encounter between Nick and Duncan took place in the context of what were to be a series of projects to explore the spirit of the Dairylea, Kenco and Philadelphia brands. At the time, Nick Shepherd was a senior marketing manager at Kraft.

'It was with huge trepidation that we went ahead the first time,' he says.

The focus for the initial project was Dairylea, a brand that was well established but due for rejuvenation and a relaunch. The event gathered together a broad cross-section of marketing, R&D and factory people plus representatives from the advertising agency.

'We went away for two days when we were presented with a number of bizarre exercises, including kick boxing, walks when we looked for things. As someone on the more conservative end of things, I had to suspend my scepticism,' says Nick. 'But it proved to be an incredibly rewarding process.'

The returns from the project were two-fold: the breakthrough in brand insight came in double-quick time.

'On the one hand we got to somewhere we would not have reached otherwise. We leaped to somewhere new and different. And we certainly would not have got there in one go.'

Aside from Shepherd's own reservations at the outset, the advertising agency was at least as sceptical about the project. 'But we were happy to support this because we wanted to make a step change,' he says. There were a number of exceptional benefits for Shepherd.

'We came away with a very good rounded view of the brand that was as true to the past as to where we felt the future lay. You could easily go into this kind of project and forget about the history, but one of the beauties of the process is that we didn't forget the past. We saw how to take what was important about the brand from the past into the future.'

As far as the brand dream model is concerned, Shepherd found that it provides a highly concentrated definition of the main features of the brand. 'In some ways it reflects what Jeremy Bulmer once said, "Oh for the joy of a tight brief". So I think that its simplicity is a real positive about the model. The brevity of the output means that people remember it and carry it around in their heads. And despite the simplicity of it, it does act as something that you can judge anything you do against the three circles.'

With hindsight, the payoff may be obvious. But it was an act of faith that sustained Shepherd through the project. 'I became more confident as we went along because different exercises were stimulating different responses about the brand from people. I noticed this in myself. I started to think that maybe we will come up with something different – but different can be good or bad. Part way through the process, you ask yourself "Are we going to get something out of this?" You don't really know until the end when you do the final exercise.'

Despite his foreboding, Shepherd found that not only did the company emerge with something that inspired a new approach to the Dairylea brand, but also that the activities involved in the project turned out to bring their own lasting value.

'Going through the process is a very inspiring experience and a good team-building exercise. By involving a cross section of people inside and outside the organisation meant that you ended up with a level of commitment that was very high. Marketing would have been the laughing stock of the company if nothing had come out of it. We would have never heard the end of it.' His verdict is that the brand dream approach is 'High risk, high reward'.

Of all the projects in which he was involved, Shepherd rates Dairylea as the first and most successful. Philadelphia proved to be more difficult, although there was a positive outcome from all three projects. 'It was something to do with the brands,' he says.

'On Dairylea, we did an awfully lot better than anything else we could have done. On other projects we still did better than we could have achieved otherwise.'

Looking back, Shepherd believes that there were a number of circumstances that made the Dairylea project the most successful. 'We had a new team working on this brand and we had a huge amount of emotional baggage to work through. It was a brand with a long history. I think it would be much more difficult to run a brand dream project for something that was only two years old.'

Aside from this, what strikes him as different about the whole experiential approach is that:

- 'It brought people together in a way that other brand development approaches would not.'
- 'The clarity, simplicity and holistic nature of the model mean that you go ahead without losing the past and history. The trouble with other techniques is that they tend to ignore the baggage and just focus on where we'd like to be.'

He singles out two potential problems with the brand dream approach. 'Until you get to the end, you don't know what you're going to end up with.' It is also high risk. 'You do rely on the goodwill of all the participants. But I don't think we lost anyone along the way. The ad agency were most sceptical, but at the end of the day, the outcome was so good they couldn't deny its value.'

For Shepherd, there is clear potential for brand dream programmes in the future. 'If I had a brand with a lot of emotional values to play with and a rich heritage, the more likely I would think that this would work very well. Great brands were great for a reason. The emotional values will be as true today, but they may have become anachronistic in the way they have been displayed or communicated to the consumer. There's no reason why you can't find what made them great. But you've got to go back and rediscover the diamond. If you have a brand in the doldrums, it's an outstanding tool to reinvigorate it.'

Building a multicultural consensus around a brand

Chris Priest, recently appointed VP Marketing Europe Digital Appliances with LG, had championed the use of the brand dream model in a former job.

When Chris Priest went to Sweden as Nordic Marketing Director, Snacks, for Kraft Foods in the late 1990s, his first challenge was to work on the Estrella chips and snacks brand. He had already been involved at the beginning of the UK Dairylea project and therefore had first-hand experience of the brand dream model. 'I could see potential for what could be done with Estrella in Scandinavia.'

But unlike Dairylea, Estrella was a multi-country project and involved working with a number of national marketing and sales teams.

Chris had picked up on several aspects of the UK project which inspired him to try the same approach in Scandinavia. 'The key things were the level of engagement that it involved and the methods used.' As an experienced marketer, he had worked with a range of ad agencies and brand consultancies and so was familiar with the spectrum of frameworks for redeveloping brands 'from pyramids to keyhole models … What was particularly important about the whole process was the experiential approach.'

Nothing else that he had found combined the same blend of involvement and methodology. 'JWT's Total Branding was similar in its intent, but felt more mechanical. I found the creativity and innovative nature of the brand dream approach appealing.'

More importantly, there was a close match between what Priest wanted to achieve once he had moved to Estrella and the way the process operated. 'The reason why I thought it would be appropriate is that we needed to harmonise the brand across territories. We had lots of different ideas, a lot of people from different countries pointing in different directions and we needed to come to an agreed vision. So I turned this project on its head. I wanted to use the brand dream engagement to get people working together whilst focused on a common task.'

First impressions of the brand dream model

'Once I found out what was involved, it took a huge leap of faith. The newness appealed to me, but there was also a healthy measure of fear and apprehension. Going on Shaman walks, the thought of getting our sales director to dance. It was all a bit daunting.'

There was a lot riding on the outcome, not least for his personal reputation. Chris had been newly appointed to the marketing position in Scandinavia and he was keenly aware that what he was proposing was not the kind of straight up-and-down brand development project that most would have expected. 'There was a risk that they would look on me as the mad Englishman,' he said. Aside from anything else, there was the question of whether the process would work across cultures. 'I found the Finnish to be far more task and results orientated while the Swedes liked to reach consensus through detailed discussion of issues.'

To get the buy-in from everyone, Chris decided that the key was to emphasise the tangible results that would be gener-ated at the end of the project. 'I did it by clearly explaining the objectives – a stronger, harmonised brand and close-knit team working together on a common cause. We also wanted a brand that we could develop into the future.' Even so, there were risks.

'I had been given the backing of the company and I was putting that trust on the line. I had to persuade people on the basis of the business value that we could gain.'

The project kicked off with a brand dream programme for the core team held in Lillehammer, Norway, which was attended by the marketing and sales directors representing four Scandinavian countries. Disappointingly, the first run-through of the programme failed to produce a vision that everyone was able to buy into. 'Even though we didn't get to a perfect answer with the first try, everyone realised that there was more common ground than they had initially thought.'

It took a second attempt before the company emerged with a complete brand dream model. Following this, two-day programmes were rolled out in each of the four Scandinavian countries to gain deeper employee enrolment. Later this went on to be extended further into Eastern Europe as a key tool for the Estrella geographic expansion. And important changes flowed from the project that had an impact at various levels of the business.

One outcome was that it resulted in the development of a new Estrella logo. 'You might think that this was a brand management thing only. But it involved a number of significant symbolical changes. The day the crane turned up to take down the old sign on the Swedish factory building, it was a sign that things were changing and a symbol of how the company was modernising.'

The common understanding, brand personality and behaviour were also used to drive new product ideas. Also, beyond these immediate applications in the marketing and brand areas, other changes registered at a team and cultural level.

'When I arrived there was a Nordic marketing team, but no marketing director. Someone was given the job of co-ordinating the national marketing managers, but it was too easy for them to talk about why they were different. The brand dream project was a tool for getting them to recognise what was similar. It helped a team spirit to develop. Historically marketing had been seen as secondary to sales and this project gave a structure, purpose and focus around the brand. Several product managers had dawning moments – "So that's why I'm here".'

Not that everyone took to the unorthodox activities enthusiastically. 'It's a bit like Marmite,' says Priest. 'You either love it or hate it.'

'There were certainly people who were sceptical and a few who didn't think there was anything tangible that could be taken away at the end of the project.' In the end, the results justified going out on a limb. On the basis of his experience at Estrella, Chris believes that 'There has to be an enthusiastic sponsor to see it through.'

Is there really something different here? Chris feels that the brand dream approach embodies a number of exceptionally valuable features. 'Although there are plenty of agencies that have their models, the involvement of the team and the way this method stimulates creativity is still unique.'

Part of the strength of the model is its simplicity. 'But everything depends on how you apply it. If you use it conceptually, it's fantastic. It's more than a few words in a circle. It's what they stand for and how they guide and focus every activity for the brand. When people buy into the emotional output that makes it powerful.'

This buy-in comes from the process that generates the words. 'It's the actual journey, perhaps, that matters most. It enables people to develop a team spirit, a common passion for their brand's success.'

He is well aware that there are hundreds of consultancies and agencies, large and small, advising on brands, many of which have merit. 'But for breaking the norm and looking at a brand from a team perspective, this is one of the best. There's no breakthrough point with more conventional approaches to brand development. This immerses you.

It's a still hidden gem that many other companies should try.'

Understanding brand chemistry of the brand

The two preceding examples show how the brand dream process and model have been applied in the FMCG world. Here, the context is quite different and takes us into the worlds of technology, speciality chemicals and paints.

David Bott is director of innovation platforms at the Technology Strategy Board, a body that promotes innovation in the UK. Previously, he worked at ICI and then as a consultant to a government department. In both places he was instrumental in recommending the application of the brand dream process.

When Bott was at ICI he worked in the group technology office. The job of the small team was to monitor the underlying technology used across the group's five divisions, the rationale for retaining individual units and how technology was leveraged and shared across the group. As part of his role, Bott was also called in by the communications group who wanted to move ICI from being seen just as a forward-thinking technology business into a customer-focused business. 'I was the technology person who explained things to the communications people. They turned to me because I had worked on polymers in hair care, paint chemicals and components of other consumer products.'

Duncan's company wrote what Bott called 'the cheekiest note' to the chairman about revitalising the brand of ICI. It was short, to the point, challenging and struck a chord. After it was passed down to the head of communications, the brand consultancy was invited to run a programme for a small group of senior executives from different divisions in the group to help them focus on rebranding the chemical giant as a business solutions business.

Decision-makers at ICI were won over by the way the brand dream model had been presented as a means of getting to grips with the brands of a number of leading companies. 'What was appealing was how the model could be used to unpack a brand. We had a storybook and could think about the examples we had been shown, including Nike and McDonald's. We also saw how it worked in similar companies like Mercedes Benz, with its focus on excellence in engineering.'

After a high-level introduction for the senior executive group, a brand dream programme was run for the heads of communications from ICI divisions and some of the operating companies. 'I think the fact that this had traction was because it involved a peer group of people familiar with the language of brands.' Following this project, the communications heads presented a model to the senior executives who had already seen how the model worked and understood how it could help to refocus the ICI brand.

'Before the model was developed, no one had a clear view of all the underlying traditions and principles of the brand. The communications group was able to use the model to show how the brand could be promoted to the outside world and internally.'

After Bott left ICI to work as a consultant, one of his assignments involved the restructuring of a division of a government department. Knowing first-hand what the brand dream model could achieve in uniting an organisation around a set of principles, values and purpose, he recommended its use to the senior executive team. 'At the time I became involved, there was no shared vision of the brand or strategy, people outside were not clear what we did.'

The resulting project involved running the brand dream programme in tandem with a more conventional strategy development exercise. Starting with an initial project with the senior executive team, a brand dream model was developed for the organisation and then rolled out in a series of follow-up programmes across the unit. 'A number of individuals certainly glimpsed possibilities of seeing the world in a different way.'

Despite the success of the brand dream model in setting the scene for a brand focus for the group and the beginnings of a culture change – 'We saw the first shoots of change' – a subsequent government reorganisation programme, including the appointment of the chief executive of the unit to a new post elsewhere, prevented the new principles from being embedded in policies and practices. 'Events moved too fast,' he says.

Nonetheless, Bott saw evidence that the approach could profoundly change the way some people think about issues. The two-day event was held on England's south coast and culminated with a medicine walk. 'One of the team who was initially sceptical about the approach came back from his walk appalled by the examples of pollution on the beach. He said that he had never looked at things quite in the same way before.'

On this occasion, the audience was comprised mainly of scientists and technologists. 'For some of the senior people in this group the process was slightly off the wall,' says Bott. 'People either get it and embrace it, or they reject it. There are some people who still rave about the whole programme and talk about it today.'

In his view, one of the strengths of the process is that it enables the emotional aspects of the brand to be explored. But he also believes that involving some people in the more touchy-feely exercises can be tricky. Having seen the brand dream process applied with marketing and technology people, he believes that these aspects of the programme often pose a tougher challenge for scientists. 'Those who are propped up by logic prefer things that can be explained rigorously. Getting them to expose their emotions and feelings about things can be more difficult.' Balanced against that observation is the recollection that for a number, including the beachcomber, it can switch on a new way of looking at the world.

As a scientist he is used to working with models and finds that having a framework for capturing the output of the process, as well as for analysing the properties of brands, is an important strength. 'When you give anyone a mechanism for analysing the world, you empower them,' says Bott. 'It's partly because the model is so simple that it is blindingly successful.' It also passes his relevance test.

'The model can be applied universally, including to us as individuals. I have a brand built up from what I do, what I've done and my values. The model works all the way up to the largest corporations.'

Deconstructing

Brands

A new way of sussing out the competition

Chapter 7

'Today, competitive advantages weigh no more than the dreams of a butterfly.'

Jonas Ridderstrale and Kjell Nordstrom[25]

The beauty of the brand dream model is that it is endlessly versatile. Once you have applied the process to your own organisation, you can use it to refocus your strategy, identify promising brand extensions, strengthen staff engagement, spin off new ventures, or reinvigorate product development and innovation. Not least, you can use it to guide your marketing and promotional activity. But it does not stop there.

After you have constructed the model for your own organisation and have a good grasp of how it works, the model can be turned into a powerful tool for analysing and understanding your competitors' strengths, weaknesses and their positioning in the marketplace. Once you understand the underlying principles of the brand dream model and process, you can apply them to deconstruct other organisations' brands and see them as you have never seen them before.

---

[25] *Funky Business*, Jonas Ridderstrale and Kjell Nordstrom, Prentice-Hall, 2000.

Nor is it only the secrets of businesses that can be unlocked using the brand dream process. Schools, political parties, public sector bodies, charities or broadcasters are all brands in the broadest sense used in this book that are built on values, driving passions and dreams. They can all be deconstructed and viewed through the brand dream lens.

By applying information in the public domain, and what you may know from first-hand knowledge, it is possible to sift these clues to create what amounts to a default brand dream model for any organisation. It will not, of course, be what insiders would produce if they did the job themselves, but you will be surprised how revealing your observer's brand dream model can be. The mere act of constructing a model for a competitor will lead to insights that will enable you to gain fresh insights, maybe even one of those 'Ah Ha!' moments. At the very least, it is a powerful way of reviewing your assumptions about other organisations. Better still, undertake the exercise collaboratively with colleagues and associates to help you reach a shared understanding of third-party brands.

The following deconstruction exercises are all based on publicly available information to be found in promotional material, websites, books, articles and other widely available sources. All we have done is to sift the evidence to see what these companies would look like in brand dream terms. So while they might not be the real thing, they are an evidence-based, outsider's best guess as to what these models might look like.

A word of caution. This arms-length exercise can only go so far. Your challenge is to imagine your way into the owners' way of thinking about their brands. Doing the same thing from the inside out would be the only way of producing the authentic article.

Once you have constructed a brand dream view of another company, you can use it to cycle through a range of issues. What market and product development moves would you expect from these companies? If these companies had looked at themselves from a brand dream perspective, would they have done things differently? To what extent do they seem to understand their own brand dream? Does this tell us anything about new threats and opportunities?

We have selected a number of organisations with contrasting histories. There are entrepreneurial high fliers, like the Virgin entertainment to mobile phones and airline group, mavericks like Ryanair, through to whizz kids like Google. Some have stumbled and rediscovered their way, such as Marks & Spencer. To show how this can work for other kinds of organisations, there is a charity, Oxfam, a public broadcasting corporation, the BBC and even a political party, the Conservatives.

I had a dream ...

Throughout the book, there has been an emphasis on the integrity of the brand dream. Problems arise when the original dreamer leaves and the organisation moves to the next stage of managed growth; the clarity of vision and purpose can become diluted or even lost. It is then that an enterprise can start to drift, performance weakens and problems emerge. Invariably, the subtle combination of traditions, behaviour and dream that informed the original spirit of the brand is undermined and the business suffers. As businesses mature, the need for consensus on brand fundamentals becomes ever more essential and trickier to establish. If not, the pressure to adapt to changing business conditions may result in decisions that stretch the brand to breaking point. The connection with the original dream can start to look tenuous. It may break altogether.

You do not have to look far to find organisations that have wrestled with this evolutionary challenge and the difficulties they have run into. In the UK, the Labour Party's metamorphosis into New Labour in the 1990s involved abandoning many long-standing socialist tenets and shifting the party towards the centre. Whether this was a betrayal of Labour's brand dream or a necessary revision of the dream has been the subject of ferocious debate. The net effect has been to blur the brand and confuse the electorate about what it stands for, particularly with the drift of the Conservatives from right to centre. Both parties have created identity difficulties for themselves, as well as the Liberal Democrats who have traditionally been the party of the centre.

With the pace of change becoming even more hectic, pressure points become more frequent, choices more challenging and the risks of getting it wrong, greater. Organisations are used to looking at the options from financial, strategic, operational and market angles. But the piece that is arguably most often overlooked is the brand dream perspective. If decision-makers made this the starting point for reviewing their options, they would be less likely to make bad choices.

As well as being a solid insurance against arbitrary decisions, having a brand dream model means that an organisation is in a much stronger position to respond creatively to the constant threats and opportunities that are raised by change.

Nike: best is never good enough

Uncompromising, competitive and performance-obsessed, Nike has always made it clear that it regards coming second as just another way of admitting you have lost. The Nike brand is about winning. The constant search for product improvement, the fine-tuning of its range for different sports

Racing towards global dominance

and markets backed up by endorsements of sporting super-stars, all underline its passion for excellence and top-flight achievement.

It is a philosophy that has zero tolerance for underperform-ance, something reflected in many of its famous advertising slogans from 'Just do it' to the take-it-on-the-chin message 'You don't win the silver; you lose the gold' aimed at also-rans at the 1996 Atlanta Olympics. Then there is the almost arrogant confidence of 'Irreverence justified'.

The same tough approach comes through in the way the company approaches the management of its business. One of the much-quoted sayings of founder Phil Knight is that 'Business is war without bullets'.

Today, the Nike 'swoosh' logo commands 45% of the American athletic footwear market, a share it has maintained since 2005 and which gives the company a stretching lead over the rest of the field. Having fought its way to top-dog position in the US market for athletic footwear, Nike is now setting out to take the battle to the rest of the world.

Total annual revenues are around $16 billion and the plan is to boost this by $8 billion a year by internationalising the business aggressively and diversifying its range of prod-ucts. Currently, about 60% of its earnings are accounted for by footwear, the remainder coming from clothing and other ranges. Not surprisingly, Nike has a strategy for global domination.

There have already been some significant changes since Mark Parker took over from Phil Knight as CEO in 2004, most notably the restructuring of the company. Previously product-based, Nike is now organised around sports-focused divisions covering the gamut from action sports and baseball to yoga. By grouping the business round specific sports, Parker's aim is to get closer to its customers in each segment. With 13,000 products on its books, there is something for nearly everyone, including shoes specially targeted at Indian cricket players (Nike is aiming for close links with this burgeoning national programme) through to those designed for Native American runners.

Nike's research and development effort is central to the constant pursuit of smarter products, be they sweat-wicking vests for Olympic competitors or Nike Plus intelligent trainers that hook up wirelessly to an iPod to track pace-by-pace performance. Later, runners can log on to Nike's website for further analysis and comparison with other enthusiasts. There are other changes in Nike's direction, including a heavy commitment to sustainability and corporately responsible business practices which follow strident criticisms of its employment record in the Far East at the end of the 1990s.

'We see corporate responsibility as an integral part of how we can use the power of our brand, the energy and passion of our people, and the scale of our business to create meaningful change,' says Parker.[26] Corporate responsibility goals are now built into the company's long-term growth and innovation strategies. This includes a commitment to:

- Improve working conditions for supply-chain workers.
- Environmental sustainability in product development.
- Work towards becoming carbon neutral.
- Last but not least, to promote a healthy society and social change.[27]

Nike shows no lack of appetite for taking on a challenge, nor setting a series of testing financial and strategic targets by which it can be judged. Despite the awesome goals it has set itself, it might just do it.

Traditions: sport and product performance. The culture Parker inherited was steeped in a passion for sporting excellence, something which first brought Phil Knight, then an athlete, and coach Bill Bowerman together on an Oregon athletics track in the 1960s and led soon after to the formation of Blue Ribbon Sports and then the launch of the Nike brand in the early 1970s.

---

[26] www.nike.com

[27] www.nike.com

Weird and colourful stories litter the company's history, such as how Bowerman hit on an improved running shoe design inspired by his wife's waffle iron. He successfully imitated the ridged, grid pattern on the shoe's sole to improve traction and reduce weight.

From then on innovative design has helped to drive the company's success over the decades, although it experienced some turbulence in the 1980s. Nike got off to a flying start at the beginning of that decade with its Tailwind running shoe incorporating Nike Air technology. It became a publicly quoted company in 1980. Following the departure of some of the company's original staff, performance wavered over the next few years. Nike relinquished its number one athletic footwear spot, having missed out on the aerobics boom. But by the end of the decade, with the launch of its Air Max range, with visible Nike Air bags, and a highly successful campaign that featured the Beatles' *Revolution* recording followed by its 'Just do it' series of ads, the company was on its way back up. Its comeback was sealed with the launch of its cross-trainers at the end of the 1980s. Having reclaimed the number one position in its home market, it never conceded that position again.

Backing up its claims of product superiority, it secured the endorsement of leading sporting champions, including Tiger Woods, Tour de France champion Lance Armstrong and NBA star Michael Jordan. All this helped Nike to build up an unparalleled global brand. Its sponsorship of the Beijing Olympics is part of its strategy to underpin its brand not just in China, but worldwide.

Behaviour: just do it. From the early days, when Bill Bowerman would rip apart the imported shoes that the Blue Ribbon Company distributed to discover how to improve on their design, there has been an intensity about the pursuit of smarter solutions. That, and working closely with athletes who shared a passion for performance improvement, helped to ensure that Nike has always been closely associated with the leading edge of performance.

Communicating that passion for sporting excellence to the marketplace has also taken the company into new areas.

Nike's Secret Tournament campaign in 2002 around the soccer world cup was its first integrated, global marketing effort that incorporated advertising, web, public relations, retail and consumer events to promote Nike's soccer products in a new way. It was, says Nike, a 'departure from the traditional "big athlete, big ad, big product" formula' it had traditionally employed.

Following the restructuring into divisions dealing with individual sports, there are now marketing and R&D heads for each area. As he explained in a recent interview with *Forbes* magazine, getting closer to these different customer segments will be key to the brand's success.

Nike's managers live and look the part of the sports they represent, which explains the piercings and tattoos on staffers in the department called Nike Skate (that means skateboards) and the preppy attire at Nike Golf. 'We want to segment and diversify,' says Parker. 'Our potential has everything to do with how well we focus and align ourselves in each of the different businesses.'[28]

As Parker acknowledges, places like China may be a big prize for Nike. But it calls for a different approach. The Beijing Olympics will provide Nike with a big-splash opportunity in a market where it already has 3000 stores and is nudging $1 billion revenues in 2008. He told *Forbes* that 'We're not going to take the Western version of the brand and try to shove it down their throats.'

A fact-finding mission that involved Nike with representatives from the Chinese media and entertainment worlds provided insights into the tensions in the marketplace. 'The creative community is looking for its voice, and we're trying to be sensitive to that.'[29]

---

[28] 'On the Run', Monte Burke, 02.11.08, http://www.forbes.com/
[29] 'On the Run', Monte Burke, 02.11.08, http://www.forbes.com/

There are some testing times ahead if Nike is to replicate its 'Just do it' ethic and brand values in niche markets and meet the bigger challenge of thinking globally and acting locally in the world's emerging markets.

Dream: irreverence justified. Underpinning Nike's growth has been an empathy for people's deeper aspirations. 'If you have a body, you're an athlete' – Bowerman's one-liner elevates everyone to a place on the path that leads ultimately to the Olympic podium. It is a sentiment that has been retained in the Nike mission: 'To bring inspiration and innovation to every athlete in the world.'

But behind the mission, there is a dream about enabling people of any level of ability to achieve their full potential. Whether this involves challenging the limits of technology, human performance, or Nike's own quest for breakthrough innovation, workplace and social improvement, there is a sense of never being daunted by the impossible. The spirit of its brand can be summed up in 'Irreverence justified', chosen for the title of the limited-edition book celebrating Nike's achievements up until the turn of the millennium. The next phase in the company's history will reveal whether the dream can still retain its inspirational power.

Implications. The big question is how effectively Nike can translate its growth ambitions into results. Despite its success in flexing its brand in its home market, Nike has entered a new era that will stretch its brand to as yet untested limits. There is the task of taking Nike into new territories, something that Parker admits will require some adjustment to different cultures and markets. Then there is the parallel challenge of making the brand resonate within the whole range of sports communities that the company wants to win

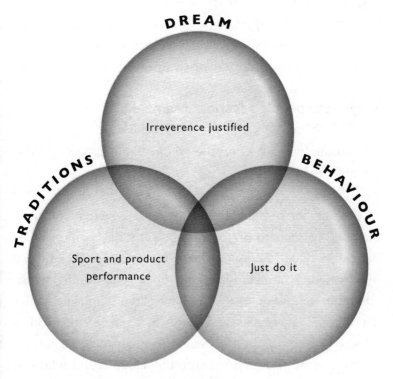

A brand dream model for Nike

over. Nike's acquisition of established brands, including Converse, famous for its basketball footwear, and Umbro, with its strong association with leading British football clubs, indicates that building a brand portfolio could be part of the answer to ensuring market ascendancy.

While sporting excellence has powered the brand through to its current position, other values around social responsibility and environmental sustainability are coming into play as Nike extends its global reach. Irreverence is being tempered by a degree of respect, where everyone from Nike to its customers, suppliers and workforce should be able to see themselves as winners in their own right.

Virgin: the people's fearless champion

This example is based on the whole Virgin group, not just the airline.

Like a number of brand-conscious entrepreneurs who have made it big, Richard Branson has made it his business to be the public face of Virgin. The two names are inextricably intertwined. His record-breaking hot-air ballooning flights and other derring-do escapades have earned Virgin's founder a poll-topping visibility and made him one of the world's most widely recognised bosses. More than that, he has an intuitive sense of how to ensure the Virgin brand works in new markets based on his 'making a difference' philosophy.

Virgin has successfully extended its brand across 200 companies worldwide

This invariably involves making a fearless and sometimes maverick challenge to massively well-established brands to carve out a significant slice of success for Virgin.

By 2007, the group listed 200 branded companies worldwide, employing approximately 50,000 people, in 30 countries. Global revenues for 2006 exceeded £10 billion (approximately US$20 billion).

Unlike some other diversified groups, Virgin has confidently played the brand extension card across a wide range of businesses from airlines and trains to entertainment, financial services and mobile phones. The group has also been clear about what the brand stands for in terms of values and what it brings to each new market it enters.

There is nothing half-hearted or ambiguous about Virgin's positioning: 'Our role is to be the consumer champion.'[30]

It is equally forthright about the values its businesses embody: value for money, good quality, brilliant customer service, innovative, competitively challenging and fun. Its boast is that one of the criteria for market entry is that it can do better for the consumer.

_____

[30] This, and subsequent quotes in the Virgin section, come from the company's website, www.virgin.com

'All the markets in which Virgin operates tend to have features in common: they are typically markets where the customer has been ripped off or under-served, where there is confusion and/or where the competition is complacent.'

Based on its public pronouncements and track record, the following are the elements that could be included in a Virgin brand dream model.

Traditions: extreme entrepreneurialism. With its origins in the music business, Virgin has always thrived on its individualism, an underdog boldness and maverick instinct for a competitive opportunity, backed up by a well-honed instinct for publicity and promotion. These qualities came through in its establishment-rocking battle with British Airways, its successful exposé of the national airline's dirty tricks campaign, forays into markets such as mobile comms and its ultimate success in building an international airline business against all the odds.

Key concepts associated with its origins are innovative flair, fearlessness, anti-establishment, entrepreneurial flair and a cheeky sense of fun. Branson has never been scared of challenging the big boys in the marketplace – Coca-Cola was on the receiving end of a typical Branson prank to promote Virgin Cola when he drove a tank down 5th Avenue before blowing up a Coke sign in Times Square.

Behaviour: for the people by the people. What to expect from Virgin is represented by its values, which range from commitments to honest and transparent pricing (not always the cheapest), delivering on promises, professional but uncorporate service, attention to detail, through to challenging convention with big and little product/service ideas. Virgin points to the fact that staff in its mobile business are rewarded according to customer satisfaction ratings.

It's fine to have lofty ambitions, but the real test, in Virgin's own words, '... is the way those values are delivered and brought to life.' The keenest test is how the company responds when mistakes are made. Or, put another way, how capable it is of living its brand dream in all aspects of performance and behaviour under all market circumstances.

There have been episodes where these bold claims have come back to haunt Virgin. One example is when the Office of Fair Trading intervened to point out that the consumer's champion had not played fairly in setting its terms and conditions for Virgin wine customers, which were subsequently revised.

On the plus side, it has collected plenty of best-supplier awards in sectors ranging from air travel to mobile phones and pensions. It also emerged at the top of a spontaneous-recall, most-admired brand study by HPI Research in 2007, ahead of Sony and Tesco (Virgin 23%, Sony 21%, Tesco 20%).

The dream: now there's another way. Given its often unconventional, in-your-face approach to finding advantages to deliver value to the customer in the marketplace, a plausible dream for the group could be its assumed role as consumer champion. This self-proclaimed ideal lies at the heart of its business development philosophy. But maybe this is a bit tame for a group that has never fought shy of engaging in battles against overpowering odds. Perhaps the 'people's fearless champion' captures the essence of the dream and makes it more compellingly aspirational.

As ever, the only thing that counts is how people at every level throughout the group internalise these, and other, values and live the dream in their everyday decisions and actions.

The implications. While the brand dream is grounded in successful businesses in a range of sectors, there will come a time when fulfilling the dream becomes more demanding. The challenge will come in living up to the dream in sectors where the quick wins have been made and Virgin becomes a more mature player. Handed down to the post-Richard Branson era, Virgin's brand dream would provide a strong set of criteria for nurturing the brand and continuing expansion into new markets.

VIRGIN

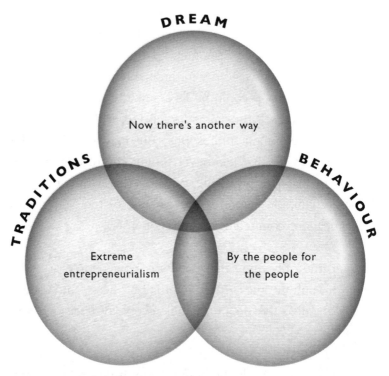

DREAM

TRADITIONS

BEHAVIOUR

Now there's another way

Extreme
entrepreneurialism

By the people for
the people

A brand dream model for the Virgin Group

Lost and found: how Marks & Spencer rediscovered what made it great

They can't possibly fail, can they? Back in 2004, so worrying
was the drop in performance that a number of commentators
seriously questioned Marks & Spencer's chances of avoiding

Marks & Spencer has had to rediscover its place on the High Street

an undignified end. '... it's in a cycle of decline and it's hard to see where that's going to stop,' BBC Business Editor Jeff Randall told the *Money Programme* as the crisis deepened. 'That's the task that's facing Stuart Rose, to stop that cycle of decline turning into a complete rout,' he said.

It was a reversal of fortunes that seemed unthinkable. Only a few years earlier, the high street chain became the first UK retailer to net £1bn in profits in 1998. No one foresaw the slump in its business over the next few years that led retail billionaire Phillip Green to launch a strenuous, but ultimately unsuccessful, bid to snap up the company.

Yet this retailing institution, with its venerable history and customer loyalty to die for, had come apart at the seams. With hindsight it was all too clear what had gone wrong. The business had let its sparkling performance blind itself to the need for change in the 1990s. Paradoxically, it had also somehow managed to forget what had made the business great in the first place.

Its business model was stuck in an era that had disappeared: sourcing clothes exclusively from home producers in the UK was no longer viable. Cut-price overseas suppliers had transformed retailing economics.

But it was not just that. The company had effectively betrayed its core customers by substituting inferior-quality, higher-priced and lower-value product ranges in the pursuit of ever fatter profits. Nor had the retail experience kept pace with the times. Its ageing stores were regarded as dull and uninspiring. Its clothes unappealing. It was nearly to be a self-inflicted disaster of its own, not its competitors' making. The store managed to alienate the very same shoppers who came back year after year to stock up their wardrobes with St Michael lines. For the first time, the faithful bemoaned the fact that they could no longer find what they wanted at M&S to reporters and on websites.

Stuart Rose, the man brought in to turn around the store's fortunes, confessed as much when he announced his 2004 recovery plan. The store would refocus its attention on its 11 million core customers – mainly women in the 35–55 age group.

'Women want good clothes ... our key task is to sell more clothes to core customers – who I think have been neglected,' he told the BBC.[31]

He knew a brand renaissance was key to any recovery.

It was to be a sustained fight back, but by 2007, the feared rout had been avoided. The company was once more back on a profitable track and the share price rebounded in recognition of its improved performance. Yet, Rose insists, there is still a way to go before the recovery is complete.

Traditions: trusted British institution. Marks & Spencer traces its origins to a small shop that opened for business in Leeds 120 years ago. The man credited with steering the store

---

[31] BBC News, Monday, 12th July 2004.

through to its twentieth-century heydays was Simon Marks, the son of the founder. An instinctive shopkeeper who maintained a personal involvement in the day-to-day running of the business, he constantly updated the way the business was run, importing new management ideas from abroad and reorganising the business when the times demanded over the decades. Obsessed with quality, he lowered his prices as profits rose to keep managers on their mettle and his customers happy.

There was also a fierce loyalty to local suppliers. Marks & Spencer's policy was to source its lines from UK suppliers exclusively. Its St Michael-branded products were made by the British for the British and strong relationships were fostered across the supply chain.

The store built up a loyal following, particularly among the female population. For decades, M&S was a byword for dependability, trustworthiness and value. Its reputation was second to none in its marketplace.

Behaviour: ultimate customer satisfaction. With the exception of the aberrations that marked its years of decline, the values that turned the retailer into a household name were excellent value for money, quality clothes that fitted a diverse range of sizes and shapes, plus well-located, well-designed and well-managed stores with a money-back deal if you were not satisfied. Customer service had been a consistent focus over the years, a value that has been extended in the Internet age to its award-winning online store.

Stuart Rose maintains that he intends to rediscover these core values while updating the brand, including sharpening M&S's corporate and social responsibility credentials with a plan to make the chain a carbon-neutral business, and signing up to Fairtrade among other eco principles.

Dream: back to the future – quality and style guaranteed. When Stuart Rose took over he was asked to spell out his vision for M&S. His response was to quote former chairman Marcus Sieff's aims from the 1950s:

> 'Offering customers, under the company's brand name a selected range of high quality, well-designed and attractive merchandise at reasonable prices which represent outstanding value, simplifying operational procedures so that the business runs efficiently and fostering good human relations with staff, customers and suppliers.'[32]

In 2007, the adoption of 'Your M&S' branding is a visible sign of a renewed commitment to customer values. Reassuring customers that it understands their changing needs, and reasserting its strong traditional values, calls for a dream

---

[32] http://www.morgancross.co.uk/the-6-steps-of-winning-strategies. html

that sums up these generation-spanning ideals. 'Back-to-the-future quality guaranteed' could do it.

Implications. If everyone at M&S had this, or a similar, brand dream model embedded in their consciousness, perhaps the company might never have deviated from its upward path.

MARKS & SPENCER

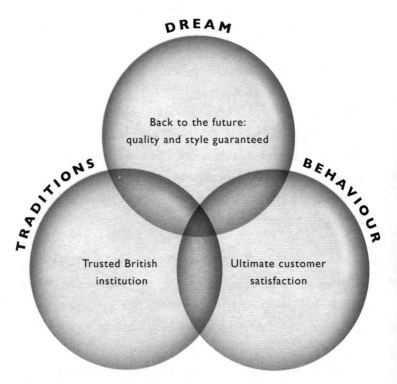

A brand dream model for Marks & Spencer

But at some time in the 1990s, the spirit of the brand was lost. The compelling principles and focus that had guided the company's rise from its lowly beginnings to the dizzy heights of a retailing institution no longer informed decisions. Yet since the dark days of 2004, there is evidence that this high street icon can survive through to the frenetic world of global competition and online trading by returning to its brand dream. What it does next will be a matter of intense interest for all its stakeholders. Stuart Rose has managed to redefine the M&S brand dream for the third millennium.

Ryanair: come f … ly with me

Michael O'Leary is Mr Nasty of the airline world and, by all accounts, relishes playing this role to a fault. He is widely acknowledged to be the driving force behind the financial success of Ryanair as well as Europe's low-cost air-travel revolution. He is also recognised as the author of the controversial policies and practices that have polarised opinion about the airline and helped to define the brand.

Admirers point to O'Leary's uncompromising crusade for low-cost fares which has transformed air travel from an élite, high-priced pastime for the few to everyman's affordable option. In the process, he has taken on governments, airport authorities, the EU and the competition with a trademark aggression to advance Ryanair's cause. In the process he has

Ryanair has become the world's most profitable airline

riled many people, including those passengers who have been left to count the cost of the cut-price proposition.

Although not the founder of Ryanair, O'Leary's association with the turnaround and phenomenal growth of the business since 1991 has made him synonymous with the airline's success. Outspoken, bellicose and rarely short of an expletive, O'Leary has earned his airline the distinction of being the people's 'least favourite airline' according to Tripadvisor's 2006 poll.[33]

In its review of Alan Ruddock's *Michael O'Leary: A Life in Full Flight*, *The Economist* notes that 'Mr O'Leary has never complained about being seen as a foul-mouthed bully. He maintains that there is no such thing as bad publicity and that the fights he picks are all intended to drive home the message that Ryanair's approach to costs is a war that has to be ruthlessly conducted on many fronts.'[34] The airline has regularly tested, and sometimes been censured for overstepping, the limits in advertising and promotional claims.

The apparent paradox is that it has managed to build its financial success while alienating those who feel bruised or

---

[33] http://en.wikipedia.org/wiki/Criticism_of_Ryanair
[34] http://www.economist.com/books/displaystory.cfm? story_id=9681074

abused as passengers, competitors and regulators. Its values are firmly skewed to financial, process and operational virtues. The airline might have got the mechanics of low-cost operation down to a fine art and demonstrated a formidable determination to fight for the routes that underpin its growth. But what many shareholders will wonder is whether the collateral damage suffered by the brand when customers and others find themselves on the wrong side of Mr O'Leary is a trade-off that makes long-term financial sense. Its hard-line style is a far cry from that of the folksy US role model, Southwest Airlines, the original inspiration for O'Leary's own low-cost approach at Ryanair.

Intentionally, or otherwise, Ryanair's brand has a rugged honesty that has left a good proportion of its customers with no illusion that they are there to make up the numbers. On the one side are those who are happy to count the savings of bargain-basement fares. On the other hand are a vociferous minority who have been left stranded, abandoned or otherwise less than regally treated.

Traditions: street fighting mentality; ruthless profitability. The company was set up in 1985 to provide no-frills/low-fares services from Ireland to the UK. From the start, it set out to undercut established national carriers. Once appointed CEO in 1991, O'Leary was given the challenge of transforming the airline into a profitable, growing business on the back of this air-travel-as-a-commodity formula. On the back of a radical restructuring of its management and operations, Ryanair has grown to become Europe's largest low-fares carrier. In 2007, it carried 50m passengers on 563 routes across 26 European countries. It is also one of the world's most profitable airlines.

Behaviour: do it our way. From the outset, O'Leary's driving goal has been to make profits by focusing relentlessly on volume growth, cost containment and low cost per passenger. There is an upside for customers from the efficient use of aircraft, flight crew and other resources. Rapid airport turnarounds are at the heart of its financial and operational efficiency. This ensures that Ryanair keeps its planes airborne for as much time as possible, for the good reason that it is in the sky where they earn, rather than on the ground where they cost the company money. The effect has been to push the airline to the top of the league where punctuality is concerned. So far, so good.

Ryanair's Passenger Service and Lowest Fares Charter spells out its priorities: 'Ryanair believes that any passenger service commitment must involve a commitment on pricing and punctuality, and should not be confined to less important aspects of "service" which is the usual excuse the high fare airlines use for charging high air fares.' Its measure of customer service: 'Ryanair has achieved better punctuality, fewer lost bags and fewer cancellations than all of the rest of its peer grouping in Europe.' Try and call customer services though and do not be surprised if all you get is a recorded message with the advice to consult the website where in all probability you have found the number, but not the answers you need.

Regular users have come to realise that the Ryanair formula is fine when everything goes to plan. The trouble starts in the aftermath of cancellations and last-minute alterations to departure times, or when passengers quibble with the way they are treated. There is simply no slack in the system for sorting out the problems of passengers left high and dry. It is at time like these that customer care often evaporates, as some disgruntled passengers have bitterly complained. They may wonder whether this is what the airline is referring to when it talks of 'the less important aspects of "service"'. Not only has Ryanair shown what a significant number of passengers allege is a dismissive lack of sympathy, it has also attempted to stifle websites that provide a focus for disaffected passengers.

Dream: the airline you hate to love. Ryanair's ambition, made explicit in its strategy document and elsewhere, is to become 'Europe's leading low-fares scheduled passenger airline'. 'What you see is what you get. I don't care if you don't like me. You like what you get' is the sub-text. However, its much-publicised lapses in customer service are the canker that taints the brand. As *The Economist* observes in its book review, '… the cavalier treatment of passengers left stranded by flight cancellations and the yelling of obscenities at people who, in sometimes tragic circumstances, make the mistake of asking for a refund have given Ryanair a deserved reputation for nastiness.' Its ambition is to cement its reputation for low-cost air travel – whatever that entails. Ryanair is the airline that you hate to love.

Implications. Ryanair is a classic case which shows that if you do not actively manage your brand, other stakeholders will take on the job for you. As it is, the brand continues to suffer periodic bouts of scathing criticism that does the airline no favours. It is, of course, not alone in the airline industry in causing grief to passengers. But so far it has shown little inclination to go through the motions of conciliation. In this respect, Ryanair's brand carries a legacy that would worry many CEOs and stakeholders in other organisations.

There is an alternative that is almost too outrageous to contemplate. What if it were to consign nastiness to the history books? If it were able to discover a new, customer-friendly ethos, Ryanair could become an unstoppable force and maybe even a brand to be envied. But that might first require a Damascene conversion on the part of its chief executive. In the meantime, the gap exists for another airline to put together a barnstorming combination: low-cost air travel and customer service.

RYANAIR

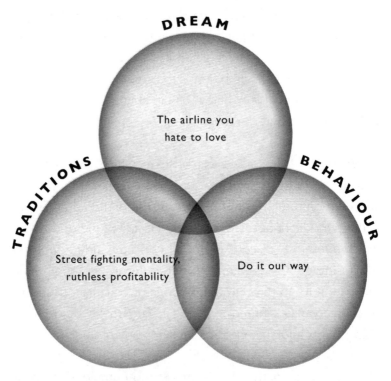

A brand dream model for Ryanair

What Google did next ...

To call it a business is like describing Manchester United as just a football team. Google is a phenomenon that has transformed the way people use the Internet. Yet in 1998 it was no more than a smart idea in the heads of two Stanford

Google is one of the fastest growing brands of all time

University students. In little more than a click of a mouse button, Google has become the byword for Internet search. As Biro and Hoover replaced generic words for ballpoint pens and vacuum cleaners respectively, so 'google' has become the default term for web search.

Astoundingly, the ascent to global pre-eminence that took other companies decades to achieve, Google accomplished in under ten years. Today it is the world's hottest brand. Taking into account financial performance and consumer sentiment, a 2007 ranking puts Google top of the pile with a brand value of more than $66 billion, nearly double its value in 2006.[35] Bigger than GE ($62 billion), Microsoft ($55 billion) and Coca-Cola ($41 billion). Google has surged ahead to achieve visibility in markets from the USA to China and anywhere else with Internet access. Its commanding brand position was built without traditional marketing and promotional support: the power of the web and personal recommendation were all it needed.

With a mission 'to organise the world's information and make it universally accessible and useful',[36] no one could accuse Larry Page and Sergey Brin, Google's founders, of lacking ambition.

---

[35] Market research company, Millward Brown Optimor.
[36] www.google.com about Google.

Despite its massive emphasis on innovation and the rapid production of services ranging from Gmail and maps to Google Scholar, desktop applications and a host of other new products, the energy of the Internet market is such that radical new concepts can blossom anytime, anywhere. Social networking of the MySpace and Facebook variety, and virtual worlds like Second Life, could be the next big things. These new services have emerged recently from nowhere. Just as Google did itself, and as other so far unthought-of innovative web services will do in the near future.

Right now, Google has plenty to ponder, not least as a result of its pell-mell growth and lightning success.

Already the company's mission has clashed with its own values. The founders' claim that 'You can make money without doing evil' has been tested in several ways. First, there is the way Google manages the privacy of the mountain range of personal information it stores on individuals and their Internet use. Its concession to China's censorship policies is another sore point for many. Nearer home, there is the spectre of 1984-style surveillance as the US government leans on the company to provide access to personal information in the name of national security.

All of which puts the company's noble commitment to do no evil under threat. Nor is that all. Google's digitisation of published material has raised a storm of controversy among those who currently make money from copyright material. With so many customers, stakeholders and partners with legitimate and diverse sensitivities, Google has to tread carefully if it is going to deliver its vaulting ambition and keep everyone on-side.

As the business expands in all directions geographically, service-wise and commercially, so do the challenges. For a company that is barely out of the cradle, it has had to learn to walk, run and fly almost in the same breath just to keep up with its own growth. As a *Business Week* columnist pondered, has it grown too big and powerful too soon for its own good?[37] As it is, the company has no option but to discover what it takes to behave like a veteran, many decades before its first employee can even dream of becoming eligible for a long-service award. The real test will be its ability to be clear enough about what the brand stands for to guide it through the difficult choices that are just around the corner.

Traditions: web search that really works; self-generating success; compelling advertising proposition. Larry Page and Sergey Brin's new Internet search engine was the foundation of the business and remains at the heart of its growth. In

---

[37] 'Is Google Too Powerful?', Rob Hof, *Business Week*, 29th March 2007.

double-quick time since the mid-1990s, the company has built an organisation with a thriving advertising revenue stream plus a steady flow of new services. This has moved the company into adjacent territory.

With its precocious approach to spinning off new offerings including its range of word processing, spreadsheet and voice-over-Internet services, it has gone beyond the world of search into areas where well-established players such as Microsoft have ruled. Until now. Convergence of technologies around the Internet has been gathering pace since the turn of the new millennium. The big question is to what extent Google, with its origins in search, is strong enough to push into this wider market. Will its brand sustain that kind of demanding extension? Would it still be true to its spirit, or would this effectively be a different business with a different proposition?

Behaviour: customer amazement. Paralleling the scale of its ambitious mission statement, Google knows that it cannot afford to stand still. As might be expected of a company born in the Internet era that has also emerged a winner from the dot.com bust of the early 2000s, the company puts a premium on being constantly demanding of itself: 'Never settle for the best' is one of its maxims.

'Focus on the user and all else will follow' is another. It points to the delivery of a consistently good user experience, based on speed of response, ease of use and similar virtues.

'It's best to do one thing really, really well.' In Google's case, this is search. However, the increasingly diverse range of products and services means that it has been pushing the boundaries of this core competence for some time. Increasingly, the company seems to be taking on the trappings of a broad-based information utility that not only harvests data in its multiple forms, but provides a channel for its exploration and the tools to make sense of it.

As a still-youthful business, the company insists that it works hard to maintain its small company ethos, despite exceeding 16,000 employees in 2007. Fun and games are built into the fabric of the organisation's Googleplex centres.

Dream: the ultimate answer. There is no secret about the publicly stated dream. Organising the world's information and making it universally accessible and useful is big and bold enough for any business. But what everyone associated with the company, inside and outside, wants to know is what does this mean? How outrageously big is the dream? How far can Google go in realising its ambition and what will this really entail? Finally, does it have a brand that is resilient yet innovative enough to go in as-yet uncharted directions?

The answers to all these questions are written in the future. But there is a revealing addendum to the 10-point philosophy on its website.

'When we first wrote these "10 things" four years ago, we included the phrase "Google does not do horoscopes,

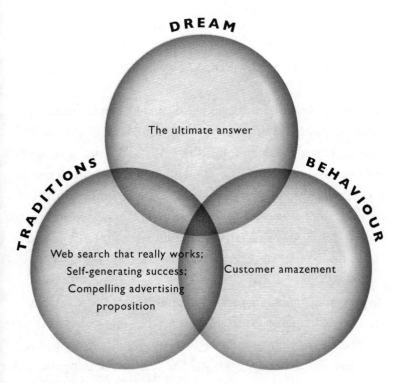

GOOGLE

A brand dream model for Google

financial advice or chat." Over time we've expanded our view of the range of services we can offer – web search, for instance, isn't the only way for people to access or use information – and products that then seemed unlikely are now key aspects of our portfolio. This doesn't mean we've changed our core mission; just that the farther we travel toward achieving it, the more those blurry objects on the horizon come into sharper focus (to be replaced, of course, by more blurry objects).'

A suitable dream might be 'The ultimate answer.'

Tough choices at the BBC

If ever an organisation needed a shared sense of its own brand dream to chart a course through a sea of uncertainty and rumbling discontent, it is the BBC. Like many a successful organisation, the corporation started life with a sense of visionary purpose. But the rise of commercial broadcasting, new technologies and changing market expectations have clouded the glass and thrown up all sorts of questions about the purpose and direction.

During the twentieth century, the BBC developed a brand that won it international respect. It became a byword for independence, impartiality and trustworthiness, both in the UK and around the world. At times of conflict, it provided a lifeline for the news-starved. Where censorship had

The BBC set the standard for broadcasting worldwide

extinguished free reporting, the World Service kept people in touch with reality. But that cast-iron dependability has received a few knocks in recent times.

During the 2000s, the BBC's authority has been tested by scandals and controversy. Most serious was the accusation by the Blair administration that the BBC misreported the government's handling of the weapons of mass destruction issue. Although strongly contested by the corporation, the spat led to the resignation of the then CEO Greg Dyke. More recently a series of editorial blunders, including the inclusion of a bogus sequence showing the Queen supposedly flouncing out of a photo shoot, and rigged phone-ins, have also left their mark on the BBC's fair-play record. One way and another, the whiter-than-white reputation has picked up a few stains.

In the halcyon days of pre-commercial broadcasting, demonstrating value used to be easy. In this globally competitive marketplace for news and entertainment, quantity, in the form of ratings, vies with quality and the aims laid down by Lord Reith are no longer the sole criteria for judging whether it is doing a good job.

Today, the BBC's activities are spread across eight national TV channels with regional variations, 10 national radio stations, 40 local radio stations and its website, bbc.co.uk. In

2007, it unveiled its plans for the digital age, including services tailored for the MP3 generation.

This expansion of its empire has been accompanied by painful organisational convulsions. By 2007, the BBC had been through several waves of redundancies and attempts to streamline the organisation. To finance its latest strategy, more cuts are on the way as it struggles to strike the increasingly difficult balance between public service and entertainment, new content and repeats, mass-market and specialist interests, all the time with an eye on the demands of the digital era.

Not surprisingly, feelings run deep inside and outside the BBC about the best way forward. There are those who accuse the corporation of selling out in an unseemly scramble for ratings at the expense of its commitment to in-depth reporting and high-quality programming. On the other side, populists argue that the broadcaster has to woo the biggest audience if it wants to retain its relevance and move with the times.

Inevitably, the BBC has to work harder to preserve its distinctive character and values and avoid an identity crisis. Whether it has managed to discover a role consistent with its tradition, capabilities and potential in a global marketplace is a matter for debate. Looking afresh at the corporation from

a brand dream perspective could help its managers to rediscover a shared dream for the future that goes beyond the
flurry of revised charters and strategy documents.

Traditions: the world's premier public broadcaster. At its creation, the British Broadcasting Corporation's unique position
as an independent broadcaster that belonged to the people,
not the state, was enshrined in its first Royal Charter of 1927.
Lord Reith was widely credited with the policies that shaped
the corporation in its formative years. By the end of the
Second World War, the public broadcast service had become
a national institution as well as an internationally trusted
source of impartial reporting. The old BBC motto of 'nation
speaking peace unto nation' was an indication of its noble
ambition. It was for many years unsurpassed for the vision
and scope of its programming, as well as the quality and
range of its productions. Today, its remit remains expansive
and demanding.

The updated 2007 Royal Charter lays down six priorities:

- 'To sustain citizenship and civil society.'
- 'To promote education and learning.'
- 'To stimulate creativity and cultural excellence.'
- 'To represent the UK, its nations, regions and
  communities.'
- 'To bring the UK to the world and the world to the UK.'
- 'To take a leading role in digital switchover.'

Behaviour: unimpeachable quality broadcasting. The assertion of high-minded values on the BBC's website would not have disappointed Lord Reith:

- 'Trust is the foundation of the BBC: we are independent, impartial and honest.'
- 'Audiences are at the heart of everything we do.'
- 'We take pride in delivering quality and value for money.'
- 'Creativity is the lifeblood of our organisation.'
- 'We respect each other and celebrate our diversity so that everyone can give their best.'
- 'We are one BBC: great things happen when we work together.'

He would, though, have been less comfortable in reading the reports of recent breaches of the code, which show that not everyone working for the BBC has taken these principles to heart. Similarly, the hostility to the continuing cuts – including threatened strikes by BBC news staff – indicates the strong differences within the corporation and polarisation of opinion. These are all symptoms of an organisation that is not quite as unified as it might like.

How widely its values are shared, and the extent to which they are embedded throughout the corporation, are open questions. Sorting out a clear direction for the broadcaster will be a real test for the resilience of the underlying credo that drives the BBC.

Dream: to be the most creative organisation in the world. This is the kind of stretch goal that should keep any organisation on its mettle. To what extent that resonates with staff, who sense a more mundane agenda focused on balancing budgets and programming expenditure, is another issue.

Implications. The BBC needs a dream that everyone associated with the corporation can believe in whole-heartedly. There is a sense that the clarity of the brand dream which inspired previous decades has been overtaken by events, reorganisation and divisive strategies. The BBC urgently needs to rediscover what makes it tick and reach a consensus about its priorities and direction. It is difficult to resist the conclusion that much of the current disillusionment and disenchantment results from a widespread loss of faith in that deeper sense of purpose that any number of strategy documents and reshuffles will fail to obliterate for long.

It is relatively straightforward to produce a brand dream model for the BBC that reflects its stated aspirations and values up till now. Having come to a crossroads in its evolution, the deeper question is whether these core goals and values hold good for the corporation in the early twenty-first century. It could be time to rediscover what the BBC stands for today, from the inside out, and produce a new dream for a new era.

BBC

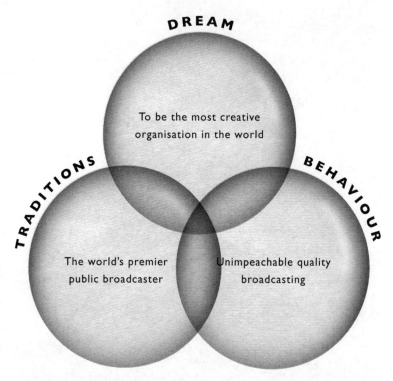

A brand dream model for the BBC

Oxfam: BINGO with an awesome prize

In common with a number of other global charities, Oxfam has grown into a substantial organisation whose remit reaches way beyond its original purpose of delivering humanitarian

The ultimate challenge: saving the world from poverty

aid. As one of the world's Big International Non-Government Organisations (BINGOs), Oxfam has become a force to be reckoned with at national and international levels on a range of global issues.

With that growth in scope, the Oxfam brand has had to grow and embrace this larger mission, scale of activities and operations. Today, it positions itself as nothing less than fighting for an end to poverty and suffering worldwide.[38]

This has meant a move into global economics, international trade and political lobbying. Inevitably, this has implications for the Oxfam brand: what it stands for, how it operates, as well as its values and position on a much wider range of big issues. There has also been a significant shift in emphasis in the way it portrays its activities. This comes through clearly in the order in which it specifies its three main activities: campaigning for change, development work, and emergency response.[39]

As a change agent, the charity is actively involved in lobbying for a better deal for poorer nations in areas ranging from fair trade, debt and aid through to democracy, health, human rights and climate change.

----

[38] http://www.oxfam.org.uk/
[39] http://www.oxfam.org.uk/

At a local level, its humanitarian work involves providing urgent aid to those affected by wars and natural disasters. Longer term, its development programmes aim to help communities lift themselves out of poverty through sustainable self-help initiatives.

Like all charities, Oxfam's success in winning funds and support depends on getting its message across and making a compelling case in the marketplace.

Having taken on this larger role, Oxfam has courted controversy and criticism. Shouldering the mantle of global champion of the poor has also increased its exposure to controversy and criticism, from the wealthy. There is no ambiguity about its readiness to take its remit to fight for what it sees as right seriously.

Some see its advocacy of freer south to north trade and over-emphasis on export opportunities as economically naïve. Others argue that Oxfam is playing into the hands of major corporates by encouraging poorer nations to enter into cut-throat competition with their peers to serve richer markets, rather than cultivating their own internal economies.

There have also been spats over trademark protection, notably when Oxfam accused Starbucks of asking the National Coffee Association to block a trademark application from

Ethiopia claiming that this would be to the potential detriment of Ethiopian coffee farmers' future earnings.

It is not only companies that have been at odds with Oxfam. Some NGOs objected to what they saw as Oxfam Great Britain's overly cosy relationship with Tony Blair's New Labour government in the UK.

What Oxfam is seen to stand for, its values and allegiances, have become as important to the charity's future as for any commercial enterprise. But as the charity's role and activities have expanded, so too have the pressures and strains on its brand. There is a continuing risk of clouding the clarity and focus that were traditionally so clear-cut.

Traditions: famine relief. Founded as a charity in England in 1942 under the banner of the Oxford Committee for Famine Relief by a group of concerned individuals, its initial goal was to persuade the British government to allow food relief through the Allied blockade to feed the starving inhabitants of Nazi-occupied Greece. Famine and disaster relief continued to be the focus as the charity grew and expanded. It adopted the shortened, now familiar name of OXFAM in 1965.

Its growth into what is today a sizeable organisation with an operating budget of $300m was based on its formidable fund-raising capabilities. Oxfam has attracted donations from the likes of the Ford Foundation and the Bill and Melinda Gates Foundation, while continuing to rely heavily on the support of the public. It has become increasingly innovative in reaching out to different groups with a wide range of fund-raising and promotional activities, including supplying volunteers for festivals such as Glastonbury through to staffing Trailwalker events in New Zealand and other overseas countries.

From the opening of its first outlet in Oxford in 1948, it now has around 750 shops throughout the UK selling second-hand goods alongside fair trade products and has opened additional shops abroad. With more than 70 specialist book-shops, Oxfam became Britain's largest retailer of second-hand books. The charity claims a 99% recognition of its brand among UK residents, thanks largely to its ubiquitous town-centre presence and extensive fund-raising campaigns.

Yet its website recognises that the public may only have a partial idea of Oxfam's mission in the third millennium.

'Oxfam. What springs to mind? Charity shops and second-hand clothes? Donkeys from our Oxfam Unwrapped gift catalogue, bought for people in far-flung lands?

They're part of the picture. But think bigger. Much bigger. Big enough for 99 per cent of the great British public to have heard of us. Because Oxfam is a vibrant global movement dedicated to fighting for an end to poverty and suffering worldwide. This drives everything we do. From saving lives and developing projects that give people power, to campaigning for change that lasts. That's Oxfam in action.'[40]

Behaviour: to fight for justice whatever it takes. Oxfam makes it quite clear that it is ready to stand up for the causes that it champions. 'Poverty isn't just about lack of resources. In a wealthy world it's about bad decisions made by powerful people. Oxfam campaigns hard, putting pressure on leaders for real lasting change.'[41]

There is similarly no doubt about the strength of its conviction explaining what underlies its dedication to the cause of eradicating poverty. It poses the rhetorical question, Why bother about world poverty? and then provides the answer.

'... belief that in a wealthy world poverty is unjustifiable, and can be prevented. Belief that injustice must be challenged. And belief that with the right help, poor people themselves can change their lives for the better, for good.'[42]

Dream: end world poverty and suffering. Oxfam's belief is that the right to a life worth living is universal and this

---

[40] http://www.oxfam.org.uk/

[41] http://www.oxfam.org.uk/

[42] http://www.oxfam.org.uk/

underpins its bold ambition to end world poverty and suffering. As dreams go, this is about as awe-inspiringly aspirational as you can get.

Implications. Although it operates under the banner of a non-governmental organisation, there are some striking parallels between Oxfam and commercial enterprises, especially in terms of branding and marketing. Like many other organisations that have grown from well-defined beginnings, it has broadened its role and scope, and grown into a much larger organisation in the process. In scale and aspiration it is far more expansive.

Taking everyone on this journey, not least the public on whose contributions it relies, is a big task, as it implicitly admits on its own website. Its challenge is to embed the spirit of its brand throughout its vast network on a sustained basis. This is a tough job, but one on which successful communication of its brand to the wider public depends. There is also the constant challenge of ensuring that the brand can sustain Oxfam's entry into new areas of influence and activity. As demanding as the job of providing famine relief can be, it is dwarfed by the commitment to fight to end world poverty and suffering. Revisiting its brand dream model could help Oxfam to re-evaluate its direction, reconfirm and inculcate its values across the network. It would also provide a touchstone for testing its ever-widening sphere of influence and activity.

OXFAM

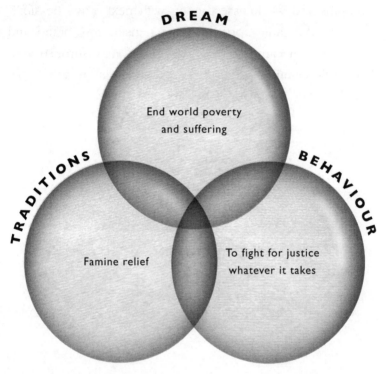

A brand dream model for Oxfam

Try it yourself

These examples from the worlds of business, public broadcasting and charitable operations show that it is possible to construct a brand dream model for any kind of organisation, whatever their activity. You could even try it for

Brand You. What should come out of these examples are the value of using the three brand perspectives to gauge strengths and weaknesses, along with next move possibilities. Use the same approach to get inside any brand and see what you can discover. The results may surprise you. You will certainly see other organisations in ways that you've never dreamed of before.

ENGAGING STAFF IN THE EMPLOYER BRAND

Chapter 8

'When we dream alone, it is only a dream. When we dream together, it is no longer a dream but the beginning of reality.'

Brazilian proverb[43]

Organisations that live the brand enjoy all sorts of advantages over those who go through the motions, or do not even try. The dividend that brand-saturated companies reap many times over is counted in terms of consistent brand reinforcement to customers, partners and others outside the business. It also comes through in other ways. People identify more closely with the business, its goals and are more engaged and motivated.

This is a highly valuable byproduct of the brand dream process. Organisations that move from the brand dream creation stage to the enrolment phase find that this is the most effective way of engaging everyone in the workforce with the enterprise's brand dream model. From a brand perspective, this is crucial since the way the brand values and ideals

---

[43] Quoted in *The Springboard*, Stephen Denning, Butterworth-Heinemann, 2001, p. 71.

are implemented day in, day out is through people. The brand behaves the way people behave.

The brand dream enrolment phase is where the brand is actualised for the workforce. In many cases, this enables the workforce to get things about the brand, strategy and the organisation that have never sunk in so profoundly before. 'I now understand what we are meant to be doing,' said one participant at a brand dream enrolment programme for a public sector organisation. 'It now makes far more sense to me. It was far more powerful than the induction process.'

At the end of another brand dream event, the creative director of a consumer goods company said simply: 'Just let me get on with it, because I now know what to do.' Brand dream enrolment can crystallise concepts in a new way that makes it easier for people to focus on their own goals.

This is also where the brand dream and HR converge. HR is increasingly concerned with the way in which the employer brand, the organisation's proposition for employees, is put over. Alongside terms, benefits and opportunities for them as individuals, there are other important factors including motivation and engagement with the organisation. The brand dream process can play a key part in transforming words on the paper into something that people can touch and feel for themselves.

The rise of employer branding

Who would you rather work for, Organisation A, whose brand and values you admire? Or B, which pays your wages reliably, but that's more or less the sum of the contract between you? And while you are thinking about those options: which organisation is most likely to inspire you to go that extra mile?

If you would prefer to work for Organisation A, and would feel more motivated to put in a bigger effort for that kind of company, then you can count yourself as one of the positive majority. 'The vast majority of employees today are looking to make a difference in an organisation that makes a difference in the world.'[44] The Towers Perrin Global Workforce Study 2007–2008, based on responses from almost 90,000 people in 18 countries, confirms that this is a worldwide phenomenon.

Despite the majority's willingness to make a fuller commitment to the companies that employ them, four out of 10 (38%) workers report that they feel exactly the opposite. This group is either disenchanted or disengaged. At the other end of the scale, there are just over a fifth who are fully engaged,

---

[44] Towers Perrin Global Workforce Study 2007–2008, www.towersperrin.com

leaving the remainder whose commitment may be lukewarm currently but could go either way.

Overall, this is massively good news. The fact that most workers want to make a difference ought to be music to corporate ears in an era when people, the business's human capital, are the only source of long-term competitive advantage. Equally, the finding that so many workers feel they are not being given a chance to contribute, or say that they are disenchanted, says a great deal about the people-management skills in many companies.

For every organisation that has succeeded in hitting the engagement button, there are four that are way off target. They should be worried about this record. So should their shareholders. Why? Engaged staff are higher performers and generate superior corporate results.

A comparison of 50 global companies over a one-year period showed that those which recorded a high employee engagement level saw a 19% increase in operating revenue plus almost a 28% growth in earnings per share. By contrast, companies with low levels of engagement saw operating income drop more than 32% and earnings per share decline over 11%.[45]

---

[45]Towers Perrin Global Workforce Study 2007–2008, www.towersperrin.com

Evidence like this is a strong incentive to make engagement part of corporate life, but it is not something that comes easily to companies that are still steeped in yesterday's command-and-control methods or are nervous about encouraging employee involvement. They are the ones who are out of step with those developing a business model that meets the needs of the rising generation of employees: a third-millennium solution for a third-millennium world.

One of the clear messages that comes out of the Towers Perrin study, and others like it, is that employees want to feel an affinity with the organisation. Brand buy-in presents an important part of that opportunity.

Once brand consciousness had become commonplace, it was only a matter of time before some companies started to see the potential for extending their brands to promote their organisations as employers. After all, if the dream and brand experience is to be real to customers, it should be the same for employees.

A recurring theme of this book is that you can take a brand perspective whenever there is someone to win over. The principle is not limited to a product or a service. It can work down to the individual level. Thinking about yourself in brand terms, as Tom Peters argued in his article 'A Brand Called You', can be an eye opener. 'You're every bit as much a brand as Nike, Coke, Pepsi, or the Body Shop. To start thinking like your own favorite brand manager, ask yourself the same question the brand managers at Nike, Coke, Pepsi, or the Body Shop ask themselves: What is it that my product or service does that makes it different? Give yourself the traditional 15-words-or-less contest challenge.'[46] If the principle applies to individuals, it certainly applies to the organisation as an employer. In today's business environment, sharpening your employer brand no longer looks like an interesting option, but a corporate necessity.

Ever since McKinsey, the consulting firm, drew attention to the 'War for Talent' in its article of the same name in 1997, business has been sensitised to the growing need to compete for employees just as they fight for customers. As successive studies show, the problem of skills and leadership shortages is getting steadily worse, not better. Successive CEO surveys confirm that the talent question is way up the agenda. At a high level, the main objective of employer branding is to establish 'the image of the organisation as a "great place to work" in the minds of current employees and key stakeholders in the external market (active and passive candidates, clients, customers and other key stakeholders).'[47] But there

---

[46] 'The Brand Called You', Tom Peters, Fast Company, August 1997.
[47] 'Your Employer Brand', Brett Minchington, 2005, http://www. collectivelearningaustralia.com/

is much more to it than developing a set of generic attractions. What kind of people a company wants will reflect a whole set of criteria, including the brand values that the business wants to develop through the way the organisation operates and behaves.

Some companies instinctively make the connection. Take Google, which topped the *Fortune* Best One Hundred Companies to Work For list in 2008.[48] It's not just that its 10-point employee proposition sets an exacting standard in the employment marketplace. It incorporates essential brand elements that make it clear what kind of people will help it to realise its corporate aspirations.

1. 'Lend a helping hand. With millions of visitors every month, Google has become an essential part of everyday life – like a good friend – connecting people with the information they need to live great lives.'
2. 'Life is beautiful. Being a part of something that matters and working on products in which you can believe is remarkably fulfilling.'
3. 'Appreciation is the best motivation, so we've created a fun and inspiring workspace you'll be glad to be a part of, including on-site doctor and dentist; massage and yoga; professional development opportunities; on-site

---

[48] http://money.cnn.com/magazines/fortune/bestcompanies/2008/

day care; shoreline running trails; and plenty of snacks to get you through the day.'

4. 'Work and play are not mutually exclusive. It is possible to code and pass the puck at the same time.'

5. 'We love our employees, and we want them to know it. Google offers a variety of benefits, including a choice of medical programs, company-matched 401(k), stock options, maternity and paternity leave, and much more.'

6. 'Innovation is our bloodline. Even the best technology can be improved. We see endless opportunity to create even more relevant, more useful, and faster products for our users. Google is the technology leader in organising the world's information.'

7. 'Good company everywhere you look. Googlers range from former neurosurgeons, CEOs, and U.S. puzzle champions to alligator wrestlers and former-Marines. No matter what their backgrounds Googlers make for interesting cube mates.'

8. 'Uniting the world, one user at a time. People in every country and every language use our products. As such we think, act, and work globally – just our little contribution to making the world a better place.'

9. 'Boldly go where no one has gone before. There are hundreds of challenges yet to solve. Your creative ideas matter here and are worth exploring. You'll have the opportunity to develop innovative new products that millions of people will find useful.'

10. 'There is such a thing as a free lunch after all. In fact we have them every day: healthy, yummy, and made with love.'[49]

This is how Google lays out its stall to attract candidates, but it is only the curtain-raiser to a lengthy process. Before they are offered a job, Googlers have to go through six to 12 interviews. The company's argument is that it recruits for success and wants to hold on to those they employ. Their success is reflected in their 3% staff turnover.[50]

Companies with a strong values set have fewer problems in treating their brand as a continuum from marketplace to workplace. Historically, Volvo was renowned as the car-maker that put safety first on its design brief. Today, the Scandinavian heritage lives on. 'Quality, safety and environmental care are the values that form the Volvo Group's common base and are important components of our corporate culture. The values have a long tradition and permeate our organisation, our products and our way of working. Our goal is to maintain a leading position in these areas.'

But claims are easy to make. The difference between authentic employer brands and those that merely utter the platitudes

---

[49] www.google.co.uk/support/jobs/

[50] Employer branding: The latest fad or the future for HR? CIPD Research Insight, 2007, www.cipd.co.uk

lies in the experience behind the words. In Volvo's case, the trail-blazing approach to both its products and its corporate culture, including its pioneering use of work groups and employee involvement, gave the company a distinctive employer brand decades before the terminology became familiar.

You do not have to be a mega company to create a differentiated employer brand. Long before corporate responsibility became voguish, Scott Bader had decided that was the kind of company it wanted to be, its culture and operating principles. Back in 1921, it had crystal clear clarity about the brand values it wanted to project in the marketplace and especially as an employer. Today, its specialist chemicals companies operate from five manufacturing sites across the world and have carried the corporate philosophy with them. 'The Spirit of Scott Bader' statement spells out its goals:

'Scott Bader companies are the business units of a larger membership organisation called The Scott Bader Commonwealth. Everyone working in Scott Bader is expected to become a member of The Scott Bader Commonwealth. Members share the responsibilities and privileges of being trustees-in-common and working the Scott Bader way, and must accept the challenge of ensuring the company is sustainable for the benefit of future generations.'[51]

---

[51] The Spirit of Scott Bader, www.scottbader.com

It was way ahead of its time in putting social and environmental goals at the centre of its culture. Today, 92% of organisations believe that corporate social responsibility is important to their employer brand.[52]

Scott Bader also made a radical statement by insisting that those who worked in the business should share in its ownership and its management.

Supporting local charities and working in the community are all part of the deal. 'We must care about all those who rely on us and respect the dignity of all people. Discrimination on grounds of race, age, religion or gender is not tolerated. Distribution of a proportion of profits must be made to benefit those less fortunate than ourselves.

As a sustainable, caring company our success can influence others to follow our example. We must help those who wish to follow. Also, while the company will not make payment to any political organisation – it will, where possible, support staff who wish to be engaged in community activities.'[53]

Recent Business in the Community awards, which are made to UK companies that have demonstrated exceptional con-

---

[52] The Future of Recruitment and Retention, Penna, 2007, www.penna.com

[53] The Spirit of Scott Bader, www.scottbader.com

tributions to the local community, confirm that Scott Bader continues to live its values. In the early part of the twentieth century, these aspirations were radical and exceptional. Today, companies that had never approached business in this way are rushing to catch up with this pioneering vision. Those with their sights set on achieving top league status are increasingly likely to look for confirmation that they have made the grade through a top position in one of the several 'Top Places to Work' accreditation and ranking systems. Accolades like this reinforce your employer brand of distinction status. It is also a catalyst to ensure that the organisation takes the necessary measures to stay ahead of the crowd in critical areas of culture and employment practice.

The *Best Companies Guide* sums up companies according to eight features:

Leadership
- Are there opportunities for the leader and senior management to listen to staff?
- How are the values of the organisation reflected in the actions and style of the senior management?
- How do the leadership communicate with the employees?

My Company
- What makes you proud to work for this company?
- What makes this company unique to work for?
- How are employees encouraged to provide ideas for the wider development of the company?

Personal Growth

- How could I expect to progress within the company in the next three years?
- What learning opportunities are available for someone in this role?
- How will my performance be reviewed, and how frequently?

My Manager

- Who is my line manager?
- Can I meet them?
- What management training do you have in place? How do managers here support staff?

My Team

- How does the company promote a team environment?
- What opportunities exist for teams across the organisation to interact together?
- Can I meet the team?

Giving Something Back

- Are there any ways in which the organisation works with the local community?
- What, if any, policies do you have in place concerning environmental issues?
- Are there any ways in which the company supports individuals in their own charitable work, and if so what are they?

Fair Deal

- How do pay and benefits compare to sector averages?
- Is there a structured pay review system, if so can you talk me through it?

- Are there any unique ways in which the organisation rewards commitment and effort?

Wellbeing
- How does your staff turnover compare to others in this sector?
- What systems are in place for flexible working?
- What do you do to encourage work/life balance and to ensure staff remain motivated?

Source: Best Companies Guide[54]

The entry price for joining the club, says The Great Place to Work Institute, is the creation of a working environment where you 'trust the people you work for, have pride in what you do, and enjoy the people you work with.' Valuable though these best-practice features might be in improving an organisation's appeal to staff, there is another dimension to the employer brand: its intimate connection with the core brand projected to customers and other external stakeholders.

According to Simon Barrow, chairman, People in Business, who claims to have coined the term 'the employer brand' in the early 1990s, the concept represents a logical development of the practice of conventional marketing-focused brand management to the whole organisation. Having served as a

---

[54] *Best Companies Guide*, http://www.bestcompaniesguide.co.uk/

brand manager for Colgate, and then headed up an HR consultancy, he is in a good position to see the potential for this evolution. This is how he sees the role of the brand manager in the employer brand era:

> '... real brand management is all about working with other functions, persuading skilled and powerful people to do things differently because you the brand manager have the responsibility to deliver a coherent offer and rationale across the whole customer or employee experience. That can indeed be hard.'[55]

There is more to ponder in discovering the secret of the employer brand. In their review of employer branding practice, Dr Shirley Jenner and Stephen Taylor, Manchester Metropolitan University Business School, wonder whether employer branding could have an even larger role in influencing staff engagement and therefore corporate performance:

> 'Can the relationships between the various strands of corporate identity and reputation, brand management, brand equity and employer branding be unravelled? Can ideas and concepts from the marketing of services and products really be transferred so easily to the realm of people man-

---

[55] Employer branding: The latest fad or the future for HR? CIPD Research Insight, 2007, www.cipd.co.uk

agement? Is employer branding a new language to express the meaning and significance of work, a fresh iteration of person–environment fit psychology, or just more hollow rhetoric?'[56]

Good questions. Although employer branding is still very much work in progress, there are sufficient clues to suggest that companies are looking at all the opportunities that the two academics outline above. Having a brand with buzz in the marketplace helps when it comes to attracting candidates with a similar profile to the customer base. But this does not necessarily make it straightforward to align the employer brand with the customer brand, as Annette Frem, Global Culture and Leadership Manager, Orange points out. 'Orange is a powerful consumer brand and plays an important role in our ability to attract and retain people. Our challenge, in HR, is to translate the brand into something that has meaning at work, and to manage expectations accordingly.'[57]

One reason for believing that there is rich potential here is that the employer brand represents a constructive response to a whole set of increasingly tough business challenges. The pull factor is that everyone is used to thinking in brand terms, not just where consumer and other products are

---

[56] Employer branding: The latest fad or the future for HR? CIPD Research Insight, 2007, www.cipd.co.uk

[57] Meaning at work, Research Report, 2004, www.penna.com

concerned, but in the much wider context of sports, politics and employment. Here are some other drivers.

- In a highly competitive talent market, every company is keen to portray itself as employer of choice with an employee value proposition to match.
- HR's continuing quest to increase the value of their contribution to the organisation is prompting the development of the employer brand as a natural extension of its role.
- In the knowledge era, human capital has moved centre stage as the powerhouse of business growth and development – one of the ways in which companies can influence their performance is through the employer brand.
- Customer-first policies call for a unified brand awareness that enables the company to live the values that it wants to promote in the marketplace.
- Engagement is seen as a major opportunity for raising performance. Gaining staff buy-in to all aspects of the employer brand is an important means of promoting commitment and bumping up motivation.

Looked at from a corporate perspective, it becomes easier to see why the effort involved in developing a strong employer brand should more than repay that effort. As a recruiter, you want the best people to beat a path to your door. As an employer, you want people to be brand ambassadors in the marketplace. As a manager, you want staff to be fully committed and motivated to perform. There are plenty of good reasons to invest in the employer brand.

When it comes down to the things that turn people on, there are a number of factors that top the list. A recent study of over 1700 people showed that almost three-quarters of workers were looking for more meaning at work at three levels: individual, organisational and societal.[58] At a personal level, one of the important factors was a strong fit between personal organisational values. There is also greater significance placed on demonstrable social responsibility. While these factors mattered most to those who worked in the not-for-profit sectors, they are becoming an increasingly important employment factor for workers in all sectors.

When these elements are successfully built into the culture, processes and management of the business, the effect can have a powerful impact on engagement levels. Penna's research suggests that there is a corresponding hierarchy of engagement where each successive level can be built up to deliver a more powerful driver of commitment and motivation.

Just as these factors are important to those who currently work for the organisation, they also matter to those who look

---

[58] Meaning at work, Research Report, 2004, www.penna.com

The factors that contribute to meaning at work

Individual
- A sense of 'self' – and the space to be myself.
- Balance between my work and non-work life.
- Harmony between my personal values and those of my organisation.

Organisational
- A sense of community at work – the opportunity to feel part of something bigger than myself.
- The opportunity to interact with others.
- The opportunity to contribute to the organisation's success.
- A manager or leader who creates meaning for me.

Society
- An opportunity to contribute to society.
- Working for an organisation with a strong sense of corporate responsibility.[59]

---

at the company as prospective employees. While top of the list of considerations for candidates are location (49%), the content of the role (47%) and the package (44%), many candidates are also strongly influenced by the company's brand. For about a third of younger workers, particularly, this is a big factor. 'The age of the employer brand is clearly upon us and the trend looks set to continue,' says Penna in its Meaning of Work report.

---

[59] Meaning at work, Research Report, 2004, www.penna.com

Hierarchy of Engagement

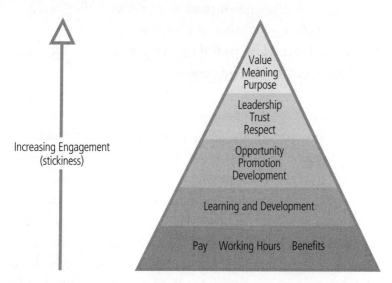

Each successive level adds progressively to the effectiveness of engagement

Gary Browning, "Why is Meaning at Work so Important?", Meaning at Work Research Report, p.22, © Penna Plc. Reproduced by permission of Penna Plc.

One of the most important implications for the employer brand is that it must appeal on various levels, not least the emotional. To measure engagement in its study, it depends in equal parts on how people think as well as how they feel about work:

- Rational: How well employees understand their roles and responsibilities (the 'thinking' part of the equation).
- Emotional: How much passion and energy they bring to their work (the 'feeling' part of the equation).
- Motivational: How well they perform in their roles (the 'acting' part of the equation).

Historically, most companies have been better at ensuring employment conditions, formal procedures and processes – the hygiene factors in the workplace – are in good shape. The emotional and motivational parts of the piece have proved more elusive, especially for those who still carry the baggage of yesterday's business and manage-ment practices and assumptions about the unwritten con-tract between employer and employee. Most people have higher expectations about what the work experience should be about. The trend is towards greater involvement at work at many levels. It is no longer adequate to provide people with the traditional package of employment conditions.

However, as Penna stresses in hammering home its point, employer branding means far more than coming up with some window dressing for recruitment purposes. There must be substance and depth behind any claims: 'Organisations, leaders and managers need to place more importance on what they stand for if they are to convince a younger generation which ranks values and ethics above promotion prospects.'[60]

Philips International, the electronics company, sees it in these terms and maintains that its success in developing its employer terms is partially down to making someone specifically responsible for ensuring that it happens.

'We started four years ago with a dedicated person for employer brand development and activation in corporate HR. This person, as well as her current successor, was recruited from a global marketing function with a lot of experience and network in the Philips marketing community. Probably this is one of the simple success factors behind the relative speed in creating one global approach for employer branding. This can only happen as a concerted effort of HR, marketing and communications.' Job Mensink, Director, Philips International.[61]

Helen Rosethorn, CEO, Bernard Hodes, recruitment and sourcing specialist, makes a distinction between employer branding and employer of choice, an early response to the talent crisis. 'No organisation should be aiming to be all things to all people – different types of people are right

---

[60] Meaning at work, Research Report, 2004, www.penna.com
[61] Employer branding: The latest fad or the future for HR? CIPD Research Insight, 2007, www.cipd.co.uk

for different types of companies,' she says. 'The focus has moved on to what it takes to build and sustain an employer reputation that binds and attracts the "right" talent.'[62] Just as brands aim to attract loyal customers in the marketplace by fulfilling their dreams and aspirations, the same applies to the way the employer brand should operate in the workplace. In this case the customer is the employee and the promise has to do with meeting career aspirations plus the offer of being in a great place to work that matches their values and ideals. Unfortunately, it is all too easy to forget that creating sticky employer brands means going far beyond drafting a few propositions and telling people how good you are.

Having chaired the UK's CIPD Recruitment Marketing Awards and had a chance to assess the 'Employer Branding' entries, Rosethorn's concern is that many companies have rushed in to branding, but overlooked the 'importance of behaviours'. They could do well to remember what has been called the 'psychological contract' between company and employee. This is the unwritten counterpart to the formal terms and conditions issued by the company to each member of staff that codify the organisation's responsibilities as an employer. The psychological contract is all about how each party feels about the working relationship.

---

[62] Employer branding: The latest fad or the future for HR? CIPD Research Insight, 2007, www.cipd.co.uk

Trust and commitment are highest when both parties have a mutual understanding of what is expected built on a mutual respect for the values of the business and its brand. Whether people perform to their highest potential has everything to do with the quality of this emotional and psychological contract. Believing in the brand is a major factor that contributes to a productive relationship. But the goal should be for both management and employees to live the brand.

This checklist from leadership and employer brand consultants Pathfinder provides the basic ingredients for building an effective employer brand.

1. 'Core Brand Definition – it starts with a clear statement of the brand essence for a company which reflects the corporate vision and values. At the same time, a careful evaluation of what matters most to employees, their perception of what the core brand stands for, the values associated with it, and their expectations will help create an employer brand description that is relevant and inspirational.'
2. 'Senior Management Involvement – employer branding simply won't work without the genuine, visible support of the CEO. They should "live the brand" as well, and become credible role models for the same values.'
3. 'Alignment with Corporate Strategy – loyalty based relationships formed with employees should be shaped to

deliver on brand promises that are consistent with overall corporate goals, and are uniform across all departments and subsidiaries.'

4. 'Empowerment of the Workers – a detailed employer branding blueprint for new HR and communications initiatives, including recruitment and retention programs, should specify responsibilities and accountabilities of key employees.'

5. 'Ongoing Measurement and Recognition – clear milestones, performance standards, incentives, and channels for feedback are essential for success.'[63]

All this brings us back full circle to the key issue: uncovering the spirit of the brand, its values, passion and the sustaining dream. Before a company can develop a successful brand strategy, be it for the market or the workplace, there has to be a shared understanding of all that the brand is about. It is all too easy to arrive at a fine-sounding statement – point 1 on the Pathfinder checklist – that looks impressive on paper but does not resonate with those who have to bring the brand to life. That takes more than megaphone communications.

Leaders who are natural brand champions have a distinct advantage here. They tend to ensure that there is a consistent

---

[63] 'How Employer Branding Can Foster Trust and Loyalty', Jay K. Gronlund, Pathfinder, www.thepathfindergroup.net

alignment between the brand, corporate strategy, and the written and unwritten rules of corporate culture. You do not have to be told what makes the company tick, you can pick it up from the way people from the top to the bottom of the organisation behave, the way they treat colleagues, partners and customers.

There is still more to be done, though. Moving from a theoretical understanding of what the brand is all about to developing an instinctive grasp of what it means personally calls for a more direct and personal connection to be made. This is why the brand dream process opens up a much bigger opportunity for embedding the spirit of the brand throughout the organisation.

Once companies have taken key people, usually a representative selection of senior managers and policy-makers, through the brand dream programme, the enrolment phase offers a way of taking the brand dream model to everyone in the workforce. This gives individuals the opportunity to undertake the same experiential journey. This time, though, the process is built round the three-part brand dream model that has already been defined through the original programme. People are not asked to go back to first principles again. At this stage, the goal is to allow people to find their own common ground with the brand dream through a series of similar experiential activities that cycle through the traditions, behaviour and dream that make up the model.

The holy grail of branding is about creating loyal customers. Inside the organisation, the customer is the employee, the living link in the chain that connects the enterprise with the ultimate customer for its products and services. Anything that strengthens that chain of customers has to be a bonus. So building a powerful employer brand makes eminent sense. Aside from anything else, it locks on to a strong human drive to identify and belong to a community. As all the research tells us, people prefer to work for organisations that mean something special to them, that they trust, and represent a great place to work. A Harris poll found that over three-quarters of respondents aged 21–35 defined success as 'finding a company where you want to work for a long time'. What better way of doing this than getting them to share the dream?

weB threats

and

opportunities

'The Internet has certainly changed the way in which you brand products, but not in the way most marketers think. The Internet is not a broadcast medium like television. It is much more of a service medium in which you allow people to interact and exchange information with you.'

Regis McKenna, chairman of The McKenna Group

The web has bowled brand managers a pitching, spinning ball. Even if you have gone through the brand dream process and feel confident that you have nailed all the key features of your brand, there is the question of how to represent these through the web. The way you might promote your brand through mainstream media does not translate smoothly to the Internet. The rules here are different. The way you reach people is not the same. The supplier–customer relationship is totally different. There are new and substantial threats, as well as significant opportunities, to brand development.

There has never been a time when it was more important for brands to be 'firm, but flexible', to adapt the words of former British Prime Minister Jim Callaghan. One thing is certain. Without a consistent and firm projection of what your brand is about, there is scope for confusion as detractors and critics steal the initiative. But there is a need for flexibility in demonstrating that the brand can absorb the feedback from the marketplace. Brand behaviour on the web can be shaped by the multiple opportunities for customer-to-customer conversations. In this domain, brands have to find ways of becoming part of that conversation, not just the subject of comment and discussion. The brand dream model remains your best assurance for judging the consistency of your messages. But their tone, the way they are delivered and tailored will be influenced by this constantly evolving medium.

There are several other issues. The web is not a single route to an undifferentiated market. It opens the way to highly targeted communications and interaction with specific groups in the marketplace. This has implications for the way in which the brand is projected. What appeals to under-25s is unlikely to resonate with silver surfers. Adapting the brand to the Internet also means facing up to the fact that the balance of power and influence is shifting. Suppliers cannot have it all their own way.

Power to the people

The truth about your brand is out there. But whose version carries most weight? Is it the corporate line that rules? Or is it the cumulative effect of the thousand and one voices of consumers and commentators that counts? Is it some kind of mash-up of all these messages? Either way, what does this proliferation of web coverage mean for your brand and its integrity?

If the Internet changes everything, how much, and with what positive or negative consequences, depends on the way an organisation squares up to the cyber factor. The worldwide web has become everyone's platform for airing their views, discovering what others are saying and becoming part of the wider conversation. So far, it looks as if companies are the ones who have been caught on the back foot by this upsurge in free-for-all communications. While individuals have seized the initiative with relish, many companies have hung back, maybe hoping for the Internet's influence to fade or choosing to downplay its importance compared with other media. But not all companies are holding back. Some have concluded that the Internet opens up a whole new set of issues as far as their brand standing and development is concerned, and these need to be tackled.

Arguably, the worst thing any company can do is to under-estimate the Internet's relevance to the future of its brand. True, the quality of comment and information found on the web varies enormously and the medium opens the door to abuse, vendettas and cloak and dagger campaigns, although these should be more than balanced out by the new opportunities and potential advantages it brings. Important though they may be, the pros and cons of the web are not the real issues. It is more fundamental than that. The Internet has become as much a part of life as death and taxes. What matters is how companies adjust their thinking and adapt to the realities of the Internet.

While the dot.com crash at the turn of the millennium seemed like a catastrophic reversal in Internet fortunes at the time, now it looks like little more than a minor disturbance in the force field of a global phenomenon that just continues to grow in strength and all-pervasive influence.

Ever since the 1990s, when people started to wake up to the fact that the worldwide web was not just another astounding technological innovation but one with the potential for rewriting the rules of information sharing and collaboration, the Internet has been slowly but surely infiltrating every aspect of our lives. It has registered in the way companies manage their businesses, politicians campaign, software is developed and delivered, writers and musicians publish their works, information of all kinds is created and shared, pressure groups lobby and consumers compare notes on brands they either love or hate. Above all, it gives all a chance to have their say on more or less equal terms. Its basic share-and-collaborate culture represents a significant break with the long-established corporate preference for a do-it-my-way command and control style of operation.

The Internet is constantly springing new ideas and those that catch the mood of the times spread like wild fire. So what has taken the world by surprise is how powerful the new web media, including social networking and blogging, has become in such a relatively short space of time. Although companies may still be cautious about how they get involved, individuals, including employees of those same organisations, have shown few inhibitions about communicating, information-sharing and socialising over the Internet. The web has become one of the great places to gossip. And the more people come back with feedback and comment, the more others are happy to air their views. It creates a positive feedback loop that becomes self-sustaining.

The Internet is a channel where people are happy to spend their money. Since Amazon started selling books a little more than a decade ago, the web has become the dominant sales channel for many airlines and of growing significance in consumer industries from electronics and financial services to clothes and groceries. Alongside this growing trend to shop online, consumers have shown a bigger appetite for comparing prices and evaluating brands, particularly by consulting peer-group opinion in the process of making up their minds about products and services.

According to the European Interactive Advertising Association, consumers are regularly lured into trying new brands through the web:

- Almost half of UK consumers admitted to switching brands after online research.
- 59% of online shoppers say that websites of well-known brands are an important source of information when researching or considering a product or service.
- They also say that search engines are considered more useful (76%) than personal recommendations (72%).
- 61% find price comparison websites a useful source of information, while 57% look to customer website reviews to help them choose.[64]

The web's influence extends way beyond the direct role played by search, price comparison and review sites. The still-evolving role of social media is opening the door to a new era in collaboration and consumer behaviour.

Perhaps it was inevitable that it has been the rising generation brought up with the Internet that has taken most enthusiastically to new media and led the way in popularising many of the practices that are now revolutionising every information-based and entertainment industry. Napster and peer-to-peer music-sharing sites have forced the recording industries to completely rethink their market strategies and thrown companies into a turmoil of internal debate which has still to be resolved. Their interest in multi-player

---

[64] www.eiaa.net/news/eiaa-articles-details.asp?id=158&lang=1

interactive gaming has similarly driven more, predominantly generation Y, players to spend longer at their computer screens.

Then there is Second Life and the virtual world phenomenon. Second Life, the first virtual world with its own virtual economy based on the Linden dollar set-up, now claims millions of 'residents' from around the world, although regulars are estimated to be in the hundreds of thousands as opposed to visitors who sign up out of curiosity. Virtual inhabitants choose Avatars – graphical representations of themselves – to move around Second Life and participate in activities. It has already caught the imagination of over 100 'real' companies, including major brands such as ABN Amro, BMW, Vodafone and Deutsche Bank who have set up a presence there to promote their brands and products, as IBM has done in association with US electronic retailer Circuit City. It has been used by the Hollywood film studio 20th Century Fox to stream live clips and extended trailers for *X-Men: The Last Stand* for a special Second Life screening. Reuters has a newsroom and the 2007 World Economic Forum at Davos devoted time to discussing the possibilities presented by the virtual world with business and political leaders.

The momentum in web innovation shows no sign of slowing. Not only have all these developments helped to make the web a more dynamic environment that meets a growing range of daily needs from shopping and socialising to information-sharing and entertainment, they have meant that the Internet has progressively become an extension of people's offline world.

Yet as far as brands are concerned, there is still a lot of ambivalence as to whether the Internet factor represents a massive opportunity, or a growing threat. Unlike traditional media, the web presents business with all sorts of difficulties. First, there is a spontaneous, shoot-from-the-hip urgency about web media that disturbs the preference within companies for measured, well-planned action and response. Second, there is the democracy of access: anyone can, within legal limits, post anything they want about any subject, including brands, in a largely unregulated environment. Third, many media are not biddable in the sense that mainstream media have been, and follow their own rules and internal logic.

Trail-blazers who have taken the initiative admit that it involves overcoming some deeply ingrained corporate inhibitions. Wharton Business School reported a panel discussion responding to the question 'Ready to sweep out traditional media?' This featured the experience of Dove, owned by Unilever, and invited consumers to create ads and enter them into a contest through the web, making an award to the winner. According to Elizabeth Poon, regional brand development manager for Unilever, 'People want to interact with your brand ... We also have a blog on motherhood. In the evenings, after the kids have gone to bed, women like to surf the web and engage in communities. So we invited moms to blog their funniest mom moments.'

Another member of the panel, Shiva Rajaraman, product manager for YouTube, the online video-sharing website, said: 'Brand marketers are learning how to put messages in entertaining forms and are giving users control over the distribution of that content.'

Other firms have also followed this consumer-involvement line. Pepsico invited people to make TV ads for its Doritos tortilla chips and submit them for a competition. The two top ads were broadcast during that year's Super Bowl. 'To give that kind of power to consumers requires a lot of confidence in your brand,' commented panel member Erin Matts, group director of digital strategy for OMD, a marketing consultancy.[65] So far, these kinds of enterprising initiatives are leading-edge, exceptional and largely exploratory.

Yet even as companies continue to work through the issues in creating their own strategies for incorporating the web into their thinking, the implications for brand management continue to pile up with frightening speed. For certain, the days when brands could walk on water have gone for good.

---

[65] Knowledge@Wharton, 31st October 2007.

Chapter Three pointed out that there was no hiding place now that the web provides a platform for comments, supportive and critical, that have a cumulative impact on a brand's reputation and performance. There is little that organisations can do to stop the inexorable shift of control from the marketer to the consumer, pressure groups and activists who provide forums for discussion about your brand. In what represents one of the most extraordinary bloodless revolutions of our times, control of the means of communication is passing from the few to the many. Previously the prerogative of well-heeled businesses and institutions that could afford to foot the bill for the full range of costly media from PR to advertising, sponsorship and paid-for promotion to broadcast their messages, now the floor is everyone's and anyone's. The web has created a universal communications platform for free through the new media of blogs, message boards, news forums, social networks and review sites. All available at no cost, except in terms of contributors' own time and effort. The floodgates have opened. Already companies have become well aware what this can mean when detractors seize the limelight. While organisations cannot reverse the trends, they can take intelligent account of what is happening and adapt their own brand management strategies to take account of the implications. Responses so far have ranged from panic, legal action and even denial through to positive attempts to turn what many regard as a dangerous new world to their advantage.

One of the first lessons that have been hammered home for many leading brands is that they are now subjected to far greater scrutiny. There is no longer any hope of concealing slip-ups, shortcomings or burying bad customer experiences. Once on the web, the criticisms are there for all to see and for as long as the web pages are accessible. From company-specific sites such as Starbucks Gossip http://starbucksgossip.typepad.com/ and Ryanair Campaign http://www.ryanaircampaign.org through to sector-wide sites like www.airlinequality.com and www.my3cents.com there are forums that collect and broadcast consumer opinion in all its good, bad and ugly manifestations. Brands react quite differently. While Howard Schultz, Starbucks CEO, says that he has no problem with the independently run Starbucks Gossip website and checks it once a week,[66] Ryanair CEO Michael O'Leary tried to have Ryanair Campaign shut down. Even if he had succeeded, it would have been a short-lived victory. Muzzling comment on the Internet is really as pointless as trying to stop day giving way to night.

From a brand perspective, the whole web proposition is challenging because it calls for a readjustment in thinking and attitudes. The fact that detractors are out there is only part of the problem for companies. The bit that hurts is their share of consumer visibility. Almost 90% of Internet

---

[66] www.portfolio.com/executives/features/2008/06/16/Starbucks-CEO-Howard-Schultz-Profile?print=true

users employ a search engine to find websites and this virtually guarantees that consumers are exposed to the full spectrum of opinion about a brand.[67] Corporate paranoia starts here.

When consumers use search to set about evaluating brands and products, they are presented with sites that are based on search-engine rankings. Since these rankings are based on popularity and the extent to which site content has been optimised for discovery by search engines, they are indifferent to all other factors. So when you search on the name of any top brand, alongside the official websites of the brand creator, its distributors and outlets you are likely to find independent websites from brand detractors, including boycott or campaign websites, clamouring for the searcher's attention. Web-search democracy means that a one-man site set up a year ago which hits all the search engine buttons could have a ranking on a par with the official site of a multibillion-dollar brand with more than several decades' history. Financial clout and market share built up over years of investment do not come into the equation where search is concerned.

'In a recent survey of a Google search on the top 50 UK grocery brands, 20 were found to have detractors in the top

---

[67] 'Search is Brand', White Paper by Market Sentinel and Weboptimiser, www.marketsentinel.com

ten results, including Coca-Cola, Walker's crisps, Lucozade, Mars bars and McCain oven chips.'[68]

Of course, this only draws attention to the dark side of search. Not all third-party comment is bad. Peer-group opinion may well include rave reviews and recommendations.

As well as enabling a new way of presenting information through search engines, another key difference between the Internet age and the previous marketing era is that virtually everything on the web is measurable. You do not have to ask what websites people are looking at to inform themselves. You can look at the evidence provided by web traffic. It is possible to tell where people have searched, what they have scanned and, if they have purchased online, where and when. One of the enormous advantages that trackability brings is the potential for fine-tuning marketing messages and targeting sales offers for specific groups, even individuals. It is this kind of precision that drives the affiliate marketing which allows online marketers to direct their promotions to websites that generate the best sales performance.

One of the other consequences of trackability is that Internet marketing analysts are able to draw some strong conclusions

---

[68] 'Search is Brand', White Paper by Market Sentinel and Webopti-miser, www.marketsentinel.com

about online customer behaviour and the implications for brands. Social networks may be less than ten years old, but they continue to grow in popularity and, from a brand perspective, play an important part in influencing opinion and purchasing behaviour. Alongside big names such as MySpace, Facebook, Linked-In and Twitter, there are hundreds of other social networks appealing to niche audiences. The front-runners claim huge audiences. In 2008, Facebook reported that it had over 80 million active users, making it the second largest social media website measured in terms of traffic and the sixth most visited website on the Internet. New networks continue to proliferate to satisfy the readiness of people to become part of an online group that is aligned with their interests.

This represents a significant development in the history of the Internet as the socialisation of the web creates a host of micro-communities united by shared interests. Social networks are likely to engender a higher level of trust than a random collection of individuals and their higher credibility rating has a number of brand implications. Just how significant these sites are in shaping opinions and attitudes to brands is shown by recent studies of their role in the marketplace:

- 'Eighty per cent of 18–35 year olds who use social networks have either chatted about, commented on or reviewed, a brand or product on an online forum or social network.'

- 'Overall, more than half are put off by negative comments, although this rises to 59 per cent where men are concerned compared with only 47 per cent of women.'
- 'Travel brands were most at risk from negative comments on social networks: 58 per cent of networkers saying that negative comments would lead to them abandoning a purchase. The figures for consumer electronics were 51 per cent, financial services 44 per cent and communication products next with 40 per cent.'[69]

In other words, what people pick up from peer-group websites can play a decisive role in their purchasing decisions. With more than one in two people put off brands as a result of negative comments, there is every reason for concern. But there is more to the power of social networks. Over half of 18–35 year olds would be prepared to become brand advocates, when they are incentivised – typically by special offers and discounts – says *The 2007 Social Media for Brands Report* from Tamar.

This, according to Tamar director Neil McCarthy, is further confirmation that social networks and user-generated content are shifting the online balance of power away from marketers towards the consumer. '... online reputation is becoming even more important.' But there is a sting in the tail. Much like the power of search to flag up both the positive as well

---

[69] *The 2007 Social Media for Brands Report*, www.tamar.com

as the negative aspects of a brand, so social networks can both build and undermine the credibility of brands, as McCarthy points out. 'Social networks are a large and unregulated channel with a massive user base, through which brands could see their good reputation built through other channels, undone very quickly.'[70]

While companies are increasingly keen to gain access to these online communities, the way this is done is all-important. Social networks are, after all, regarded as the networkers' territory, not the province of corporates. But while the social media crowd are not keen on seeing advertisements everywhere, they are prepared to have a closer relationship with favoured suppliers. This is McCarthy's advice. 'The first step is to understand how your brand is talked about in the social media space, and then decide what the best way of targeting a certain group of consumers is. The approach preferred by the consumer is clear: brand owners must look to "befriend" consumers on social networks rather than advertise to them, and the best way for them to do this is by offering discounts and special offers.'

Currently, everyone exploring the use of social media recognises that the rules are somewhat different from those that apply in traditional mainstream media, but more marketers are coming round to the conclusion that social

---

[70] *The 2007 Social Media for Brands Report*, www.tamar.com

networks present a major opportunity, given that they can work out how best to use them. A recent survey of 500 marketers conducted by Reveries.com about online social networks as a marketing medium revealed that 39% regarded their potential as 'big' while a further 18.4% rated it as 'huge'. At the same time, several were alive to the fact that heavy-handed advertising and traditional marketing techniques were not appropriate. Commenting on what these findings mean for marketers, Rodney Mason, chief marketing officer and managing director of consultancy Hawkeye, says:

> 'It means your best and worst customers now have a greater share of trusted voice than you can amass through conventional media. Your brand is quickly becoming what they deem it to be – hero, villain or otherwise.'[71]

It is the control issue that causes marketers most disquiet. Just as two aspects of the Internet – search and social networks – expose brands to both praise and criticism in equal measure, the same is true of another rapidly growing web phenomenon – the blog, a personal, online journal that is regularly updated and that anyone can read on the web. Some are highly niche in their appeal. Many are concerned with the big issues of the day.

---

[71] Cyberspace Odyssey, www.reveries.com

Most commonly they are posted by individuals or by journalists as part of a publication's or broadcaster's sites. By their very nature, they tend to be opinionated. Their quality is mixed. The best are stimulating and provocative, the worst are rants. Typically they major on putting a strong case for or against an issue. According to Technocrati, which tracks and monitors blogs and blogging, 104,788 of the 112.8 million blogs out there were on branding as of mid-2008.[72] 'Blogs are powerful,' says Technocrati, 'because they allow millions of people to easily publish and share their ideas, and millions more to read and respond. They engage the writer and reader in an open conversation, and are shifting the Internet paradigm as we know it.'

The level of activity is frenetic. Technocrati's figures show that there are over 175,000 new blogs every day with updates registering over 1.6 million posts per day, or over 18 updates a second.

Some companies have been tempted to cheat the system and concealed their identity behind a fictitious persona, typically a delighted customer. But as the Word of Mouth Marketing Association's (WOMMA's) *Ethical Blogger Contact Guidelines* point out, this is not just unethical – it also backfires when the deception is revealed, as it invariably

---

[72] http://technocrati.com/

is. At the core of WOMMA's guidelines is the need for full disclosure of identity, affiliations and interests. It also calls for the observance of community rules on blogging practices. While there is nothing in the guidelines that should come as a surprise, the bigger question is whether companies stand to achieve far more in terms of attitudes to their brands by engaging openly with their audiences. When it comes to taking a reality check on a brand's standing, there has never been a medium that offers the chance to gather more instant and spontaneous feedback than the web.

Take Brandtags, an ingenious, fun proposition that provides food for thought for brand managers. It invites people to register their responses to a brand through a simple word association game.

'The basic idea of this site is that a brand exists entirely in people's heads. Therefore, whatever it is they say a brand is, is what it is. 1.1 million+ tags and counting.'[73]

You can play the game a number of ways, including viewing a cloud of responses that have been collected for a given brand and then guessing what it is. Or you can choose a brand and then its associated tags. Either way, it gives a new

---

[73] http://www.brandtags.net/blog/

spin to brand perception and another way of decoding the meaning of brands in the marketplace.

Brandtags also serves to underline the seemingly endless variety of ways in which the Internet reflects, shapes and influences brands. Perhaps one of the hardest things for companies to accept is that most social and interactive media are unregulated and, to a much greater degree than mainstream media, uncontrollable. Yet they do present opportunities for brand building that some companies have already started to explore. But to benefit from these channels, companies need to develop a new mindset and fresh tactics that mesh with the rules of web custom and practice.

If brands no longer have the whip hand on the Internet, there are still actions that can be taken to support and build their brands on the web. Market Sentinel provides this advice to help brands minimise the risks they face on the Internet, including:

- Auditing and monitoring the threats to their interests.
- Ensuring their web presence reflects their message.
- Optimising their web presence for usability.
- Making their web presence search engine friendly.
- Ensuring that 'brand detractors' are responded to, or out-marketed.
- Creating and optimising a corporate blog.

- Using search engines for tactical 'audibility'.
- Benchmarking customer loyalty against the competition.[74]

While much of this is web-specific, one point on the checklist – ensuring the web presence reflects the brand message – comes back to the heart of the brand enigma proposition. Unless you are completely confident about your brand, its inner spirit and all that it stands for, then the risks of mis-understanding, misrepresentation and distortion will be amplified on the web. There will always be a polarization of opinion about any brand. All the more reason for putting the effort into ensuring that the brand is well defined and understood throughout the organisation. That way, companies stand a much better chance of ensuring that any messages that get through on the web are likely to represent the brand as faithfully as possible. This need to ensure consistency and definition is something that is picked up by Scott Bedbury, founder of Brandstream, formerly worldwide advertising director, Nike and chief marketing officer at Starbucks:

'We often underestimate how long brands can hold on to a negative association, even if it's just water-cooler talk about a car that continually breaks down. The web has

---

[74] 'Search is Brand', White Paper by Market Sentinel and Webopti-miser, www.marketsentinel.com

increased the consuming public's ability to rant or rave about a company or service. Smart companies now recognize the necessity of being responsive to the criticisms, in real-time, and of making sure the brand is consistent – and is as good as it can be – wherever it shows up, and even after the sale has been made.'[75]

How those messages are communicated on the web needs to reflect an understanding of what makes people join online networks, and subscribe to blogs and forums, before marketing adopts its strategy to take advantage of this new medium.

A key motivator for many people that join social networks is the buzz of belonging to a community that shares the same social or educational background, profession, sporting interests, pastimes or hobbies. Networks, both offline and online, fulfil a number of basic human needs that extend from a sense of belonging and inclusion to gaining and supplying advice, help, recognition, friendship and simply talking to other like-minded people and exchanging views. From a marketer's or brand manager's perspective, social networks and forums open up a number of opportunities.

Playing the role of expert adviser is one. Each year WOMMA makes awards to companies that have run outstanding

---

[75] 'Brand New Branding', Fast Company, July 2001.

programmes that apply the word-of-mouth and networking principles in their campaigns. In 2007, the winners included Quicken Loans for a programme that involved partnering with Yahoo! Answers to answer the public's questions about home loans. The rule Quicken Loans set was: 'Answer the question. Don't tell them how great Quicken Loans is. Don't tell them how they will benefit from our products. Don't tell them anything except what they ask.' In other words, resist the temptation to turn the session into a sales pitch, just give them the information they want.

Doing otherwise would not have gone down well as Yahoo! Answers is a community-driven knowledge market website that rewards users for posting questions and answers on dozens of subjects. To encourage participation, the site gives members the chance to earn points for asking or answering questions, as well as having their answer chosen as the 'best answer' by the asking user. Under the avatar 'Home Loan Guru', Quicken Loans' experts regularly answer questions asked by members of the Yahoo! Answers community in the Mortgage and Real Estate categories of Yahoo! Answers. The Guru's answers are recognised among the leaders in those categories in terms of quality and percentage of best answers chosen by the Yahoo! Answers community.[76]

[76] https://www.quickenloans.com/about/press-room/quicken-wins-wommie-award

Becoming part of the conversation in this way is one way in which brands can raise their profile on the web by playing by the new social network rules. Another way for brands to get on the inside track is to adopt the conventions, format and practices of social networks themselves. Another winner of a 2007 WOMMA award was Affinitive's American Skiing Company: MyA41.com Passholder Community campaign. This involved the creation of an online social networking site for its All for One season pass holders. Around 4000 users signed up to, and posted photos, stories, ski tips and videos on the site and spread the word about the pass.[77]

Or you can mix it in the virtual networking world, as in the case of the Second Chance Tree Project Takes Reforestation from Virtual World to Physical Worlds campaign. For 300 Linden dollars (or about 1 US dollar), visitors to the virtual world Second Life purchase and plant one of 10 species of trees on a designated island in the virtual community. That triggered Plant-It 2020, a non-profit organisation founded by the late singer John Denver, to plant the same species of tree in the endangered rainforest to which it is indigenous. The programme won the attention of thousands of Second Life inhabitants and was the only social media initiative among 50 finalists in the $5 million American Express Members Project competition.[78]

---

[77] http://womma.org/

[78] http://www.secondchancetrees.org/news.html

What all these examples indicate is that it is possible to get closer to customers in a completely new way that only the web can enable. They also underline the fact that the nature of social media calls for a different style of give-and-take interaction. What it comes down to in Market Sentinel's judgement are three musts:

- 'Listen to the conversations that people are having about your brand, the brands of your competitors and the issues that you both address.'
- 'Ask yourself how you can be useful to those conversations, either by making changes to your product or service, or by offering information or interaction.'
- 'Engage – and keep listening to check how you are doing!'[79]

Engagement, particularly, can be a valuable means of promoting loyalty and, in view of all the research into online customer behaviour, stemming defections to competitors. Customer engagement on the web needs to take advantage of the unique characteristics of the medium, including user-generated content. Encouraging customer contribution, for example like Dove's mums campaign or Pepsi's design-an-ad project, can be turned into an important differentiator.

---

[79] www.marketsentinel.com/blog/

So, too, can tapping into consumers' knowledge and enthusiasm to improve product development.

The web can be, by turns, an exhilarating and exasperating place for brand owners. How they react will have a great deal to do with whether they are glass half-full or half-empty people by nature. With rules and operating principles that are different from the mainstream environment, it nonetheless defies businesses to join in. The stark choice is to choose an active or passive role in cyberspace. Involvement is no longer an option. It has already been decided for you.

These are the ways in which brands are exposed and what they can do about it:

- Coverage, good and bad, from customers, commentators and other third parties. Here companies can do a great deal through judicious participation in social media from blogs to social networks.
- Search invisibility, particularly troublesome where the official website is nowhere to be seen but detractors come top of the list. Search engine optimisation and paying attention to what should be bread-and-butter website maintenance should counter this.
- Brand confusion: just as nature abhors a vacuum, others will fill in the gaps for themselves if you are not clear

and confident about your brand. The antidote is brand self-knowledge backed up with constant reinforcement of the dream, traditions and behaviours, not only through official sites but through contributions to relevant blogs and networks.

Bringing the brand dream model into the Internet era creates a new range of opportunities for spreading the word in the marketplace. Because it is two-way, it also offers new ways of gathering market feedback. Be part of the revolution.

AN INSPIRATIONAL
APPROACH TO INNOVATION

CHAPTER 10

in·no·va·tion

Function: noun

Date: 15th century

1: the introduction of something new

2: a new idea, method, or device: novelty[80]

Describing something that has been subjected to a tweak as an innovation is an act of self-deception. It may add up to an important improvement or an enhancement and be extremely valuable. But it is not innovation. Grasping the significance of this point is of life-and-death importance for any organisation that is concerned about its future. Of course, you want to know why the insistence that innovation is different from other kinds of changes. You may already be getting irritated at what you see as inconsequential hair-splitting. Here is a simple parable that gets to the heart of what the fuss is all about.

---

[80] www.merriam-webster.com/dictionary/innovation

Imagine you are sitting in front of two computer screens, each with an image of Picasso's 1913 cubist composition *Man with a guitar.* The two screens show the same picture. You look at them carefully and conclude at this stage that they are, indeed, identical. Then you are told that one is a faithful image of the original while the other is a faithful image of a copy of the same picture.

Armed with this knowledge, you are asked to look again. You start to scrutinise the two images more carefully for subtle variations in the proportions of the composition, the tone qualities of the colours and other technical painterly details. In the end, you convince yourself that there are nuances that betray the copy from the original. Or you may conclude that the copy is, in its own way, a masterpiece of forgery. But this is not the heart of the matter.

Only when you are invited to reflect on how the two versions were created does it dawn on you that what you are looking at is not so much two look-alikes as the end result of two very different processes.

When Picasso started work, he had no way of knowing exactly what the finished painting would look like. It was destined to be a never-before-seen original that was created out of his imagination and skills as a painter. He worked without a predetermined notion of the end point. On the other hand, the copyist knew exactly what had to be produced: the best possible reproduction of an original. There was no room for imagination, but stiff demands on his ability as a craftsman. Faking, however skilful, is not the same as making. They are quite different in kind and draw on different capabilities. Exactly the same principles come into play with any kind of innovation in a business or other context. They apply equally there, not just in the art world. Producing a breakthrough, or something that is strikingly new, does not start with adapting something that has already been created. Innovation is not an exercise in replication. That is why creation – you have guessed it – starts with the infamous blank sheet of paper. Like Picasso, you are not working towards a preordained end point. Instead the destination is out there somewhere, but you will not recognise it until you arrive.

Everything depends on the creative process. No one can predict what form, shape or colour an innovative concept is going to take because the boundaries have been deliberately removed and the only terms of reference are provided by creative imagination. So true innovation is unpredictable, often exciting, sometimes unsettling, and involves a degree of risk. Ultimately, though, it can be highly rewarding. At this point you might be saying, 'OK. Even if I go along with this, this is a business, not an art studio. We are not artists or creators, so why should we expect to come up with some kind of masterpiece?' At this stage, be patient. Just indulge us with a willing suspension of belief for the moment. These and related points deserve, and will receive, answers a bit further on. Suffice it for now that the brand dream model and associated process both have something important, dare we say innovative, to offer companies in discovering better ways of meeting the innovation challenge.

The blocks to effective innovation

At this point, though, it would be useful to look at some of the practical realities that companies currently face. First of all, the business world, and CEOs globally, recognise that innovation is crucial for business futures. Not surprisingly, since innovation has made an impact on almost every department of our daily lives. The in-your-face evidence has made it impossible to ignore the leading role that innovation has played in shaping markets and the contemporary worlds of work and leisure. Over the past 25 years or so, there has been an upsurge in major inventions in virtually every domain, from medicine and space travel to electronics. A good number of these, such as mobile phones, personal computers and new entertainment media, have given birth to whole industries and, for those with an eye on the main chance, created fortunes for market leaders.

In talking to the top managers in companies from the Far East to Europe, the USA and everywhere in between,

PriceWaterhouseCoopers found that companies are well aware that this is a discipline that they must master. 'Innovation is seen as a major contributing factor in an organisation's sustainable performance. For the mature economies it will become a critical competitive tool in the years ahead. For successful innovation both supporting infrastructure (e.g. R&D investment) and shared experimentation (e.g. people creativity) is required.'[81] We would go further. Unless companies master what true innovation entails and how they can tap into the creativity of people, then all the commitment of resources in the world will not help them to hit the jackpot.

If you want evidence that innovation and winning go together, you can see the close link between innovation and brand performance. *Business Week* with the Boston Consulting Group carries out an annual survey of the world's most innovative companies. This is based on a weighted ranging that takes into account the votes of senior managers as well as the actual financial performance of the companies. The fact that Apple and Google have occupied the top two slots since the annual survey started in 2006 also underlines the fact that the biggest brands are also leading innovators. This only serves to point up the gulf between those at the top of the league and those who trail in their

---

[81] Managing people in a changing world. Key trends in human capital. A global perspective – 2008. PriceWaterhouseCoopers.

wake. As it is, many companies, even those that used to have a decent track record, are now struggling to find their form.

Consumer goods companies have a long record of being serial new-product developers. But this does not necessarily make them great or successful innovators. Despite having a higher-than-average awareness of the importance of innovation to their brands, consumer sector companies have started to churn variations of existing ranges rather than launch innovative breakthrough products and services. Not surprisingly, their returns have been poor.

What these moves typically represent are incremental changes that involve making existing products crunchier, smoother, bigger, smaller, multi- instead of mono-coloured – in other words to look new without actually offering the customer anything significantly different. Breakthrough innovation this is not. Apart from anything else, too much of this sort of thing is actually counter-productive and drags performance down. By constantly making minor enhancements and changes you run the risk of over-extending your brand and failing to generate the exciting growth in performance that can be the real prize from genuine innovation. Breakthroughs are about new markets, significant brand transformations and bold strokes that will put clear blue water between you and the competition, take the market by storm and produce sparkling results for shareholders.

This is what the Polaroid Corporation achieved with the world's first self-developing-film camera over 50 years ago. 3M's Post-It Note was another inspired product, launched in the late 1970s. Then in the 1980s, Apple's point-and-click operating system was the key innovation that set the Mac family of computers apart from the Micro-soft-powered machines of the time. Another mould-breaker was Southwest Airlines, which redefined air travel for the masses and became the role model for the low-price airline revolution.

In the case of Polaroid, the breakthrough was technology-enabled. Post-Its were a combination of new adhesives and serendipity in the application of what was originally a novel solution in search of a problem to solve. Innovations that underpin successful brands are not necessarily just product-related. They may involve ideas that transform operations in such a way as to enable a completely new proposition to be brought to market. The low-cost airline formula is an example.

If you take another look at *Business Week*'s top 20 most innovative companies, it shows that while Apple is rated for its product innovation, in Google's case innovative customer experience wins it its top rating. Other top 20 performers have earned their place for something else again. Process innovators include Toyota, Procter & Gamble, IBM and

General Electric. Others rated for their new product record include Sony, Nintendo and Boeing.[82]

Brands that successfully break into fresh markets, or cross category boundaries on the back of significant innovations, are always going to scoop the big prizes. While this is always going to involve more effort than going through the motions to repackage or redesign existing products, the question remains as to why more companies are not flexing their innovation muscles. It is obviously easier to take the lazy route to produce something 'new'. In some cases, though, companies have lost the plot, lulled into the delusion that what used to work for them will always produce the goods.

This is why, after taking a closer look at the consumer sector, McKinsey issued not so much a 'could-do-better' report as a 'will-never-innovate-successfully' verdict unless these companies shake up their ideas and practices.

The consultants found that businesses that had excelled at product development in the past had got stuck in a rut of tried-and-tested methods that had passed their sell-by date. Either as a result of inertia or risk aversion, they had simply

---

[82] http://bwnt.businessweek.com/interactive_reports/innovative _companies/?chan=magazine+channel_special+report

failed to upgrade their approach and methods. According to McKinsey, that was the main reason why the innovation record of consumer companies had fallen off sharply. 'Existing methodologies have turned into orthodoxies: established ways of doing business that reinforce the status quo and hinder the adoption of novel, tailored, and flexible approaches to innovation.'[83]

Notwithstanding this poor track record, there is a strong incentive for being innovative about innovation: breakthroughs generate bigger returns, according to the consultants' findings, up to six times more than companies reap from minor product modifications.

There are all sorts of shortcomings in the way the process is currently handled. Consumer companies have become prisoners of received wisdom about how the whole process should work. They have failed to register that what worked yesterday no longer does the trick today. Here are some of the ways in which companies are letting themselves down.

- Much innovation starts and finishes within the preset bounds of existing business models and categories according to McKinsey's study. So companies are doomed

---

[83] Reinventing innovation at consumer goods companies, *McKinsey Quarterly*, November 2006.

to tread the same well-worn paths before they begin. There is no clean sheet or open brief to allow serious creativity. It is the difference that sets the makers aside from the fakers.

- There is also a slavish reliance on focus groups that remain at the heart of many companies' efforts to generate insights they badly feel they need to gain. Sitting people down round a table with a cup of tea to discuss their ideas, expectations and preferences is never ever going to be anything but a dull and uninspiring exercise for everyone involved. Despite this fact, focus groups are still used as one of the bread-and-butter means of gaining customer-driven insights. There are much better ways of getting inside consumers' heads.
- Culturally, companies have all kinds of hang-ups and unwritten rules that are stifling and counter-productive. A whole set of conventions have grown up with brand management. One of the most limiting is the notion that innovation is the exclusive province of those with 'creative' or 'developer' in their job titles. This is nonsense. Anyone from the cleaner to the receptionist to the chief executive is capable of sparking valuable ideas that can be turned into innovative concepts.

Compared with creating a new gloss for an old product, this is always going to be more demanding. But there is plenty of reason to believe that everyone has more potential for intuitive-led creativity than they think.

As Malcolm Gladwell argues in his book *Blink*,[84] the lightning reactions that lead people to arrive at instinctive decisions bypass the cumbersome processes of deductive logic. In a blink of an eye, we decide that this candidate is right or wrong, we like or loathe someone, that this or that is the right option. While we might subsequently rationalise this instant judgement, our internal supercomputer has already processed the essential information to produce an answer for us. '... we are innately suspicious of this kind of rapid cognition. We live in a world that assumes that the quality of a decision is directly related to the time and effort that went into making it.' His thesis is the counter to this assumption. '... decisions made very quickly can be every bit as good as decisions made cautiously and deliberately.'[85]

The blink phenomenon is just one example of the power of unconscious information processing. Recognise and accept the wisdom of this basic human faculty and you have taken the first step to making better use of this capability.

Psychological profiling has also helped to make people aware that we are capable of operating in different modes. Anyone who has taken the Myers Briggs or similar assessment test will know that we all lie somewhere on a spectrum between extraversion and introversion, sensing and intuition,

---

[84] *Blink*, Malcolm Gladwell, Allen Lane, 2005.
[85] Ibid, p. 14.

thinking and feeling, judgement and perception. These tests only indicate our preferences for particular ways of using our range of faculties. It does not mean that people who lean more towards the feeling end of the spectrum are not also capable of analysis, or vice versa.

Some people move effortlessly between what appear to be polar opposites and possess capabilities that bridge very different worlds. Renaissance men like Michelangelo and Leonardo da Vinci turned their minds and hands to both technical projects and artistic ventures with equal brilliance. The challenge is to discover the Renaissance man or woman inside all of us.

Despite these early role models, the West has preferred to draw strong lines of differentiation between the scientific method and other ways of knowing and expression. So the arts and sciences are seen as opposites. By contrast, underlying Chinese philosophy, art, science, medicine and religion is the concept of Yin and Yang, two opposing yet simultaneously complementary aspects that underpin life, the universe and everything. Conceptually, they have less difficulty in reconciling opposites or seeing heaven and earth as part of one continuous whole as opposed to two separate entities.

The reality is that this division between analytical and intuitive modes of knowing, arts and science, is artificial and limiting. Particularly where innovation is concerned. Business is based on command-and-control systems. Innovation, by contrast, is a messy, unstructured process. Creativity cannot be marshalled like some kind of transactional process, but must be nurtured using other methods.

Google, for one, recognises that coaxing creativity from people requires a different approach. Thus all Google engineers are encouraged to spend up to 20% of their working week on their own pet projects. The company claims that services such as Gmail, Google News, Orkut and AdSense have sprung from this practice of encouraging personal enterprise.[86] In fact, half of its new product launches originated from the 20% innovation initiative according to the company.

The wisdom of creating different rules for innovation is confirmed by the compelling evidence that creativity is not something that you can squeeze into a 9–5 office-bound timeframe. Many of the best ideas come at odd times: Pythagoras' Eureka! when he formulated the theory of displacement was when he was taking a bath. There are many examples of dream-induced discoveries:

---

[86] 'What's it like to work in Engineering, Operations, & IT', www.google.com/support/jobs/bin/static.py?page=about.html&about=eng

- It was a dream-inspired experiment that became the foundation for Dr Otto Loewi's theory of chemical transmission of the nervous impulse that ultimately led to a Nobel Prize. Dr Loewi said: 'Most so called "intuitive" discoveries are such associations made in the subconscious.'[87]

- On two separate occasions, the chemist Frederick Kekulé dreamed his way to important discoveries: his structural theory of chemistry and the form of the benzene molecule.

- The solution to a key design barrier that enabled him to successfully develop the sewing machine in 1845 came to Elias Howe in a dream.

- One night Robert Louis Stevenson dreamed the plot of Dr Jekyll and Mr Hyde, announcing to his wife the next morning, 'I have got my shilling-shocker.'

- 'I woke up with a lovely tune in my head. I thought, "That's great, I wonder what that is?"' Once he had written down what he had heard, Paul McCartney had composed Yesterday.[88]

So far from being the product of hard-wired processes and practices, many scientific and artistic breakthroughs and innovations can be traced back to this mysterious world of unconscious mental activity.

---

[87] http://www.brilliantdreams.com/product/famous-dreams.htm
[88] http://www.brilliantdreams.com/product/famous-dreams.htm

Other studies of creativity have shown that the most promising conditions for coming up with something original, different and inspired are when someone is relaxed, in inspiring surroundings and having fun. Humour is another method that produces results.

According to John Morreall, a professor at the US College of William and Mary and the founder of Humorworks, a consulting firm that has worked with the likes of AT&T, Cisco Systems, IBM and Time Warner, laughing is not the only consequence of humour. His latest book *Funny Business* was written with *New Yorker* cartoon editor Bob Mankoff.

Morreall explains why humour opens the door to creativity.

'Humour makes us think more flexibly. People who think funny do better on creativity studies. To put it really simply, humour loosens up your brain to think of more possibilities and be more open to the wild and wacky ones. There is a guy at the State University of New York at Buffalo named Roger Firestien who has a centre for the study of creativity. When he teaches brainstorming, he says you should put a joker in the group – somebody who will come up with preposterous ideas. Very often that will stimulate people to come up with ideas that will work.'[89]

---

[89] 'Why You Should Include a Joker in Every Brainstorming Session', Kermit Pattison, FastCompany.com, November 2007.

To help companies maximise the conditions for success, we have developed the 'innovation tunnel' to help people find the inspiration for breakthrough discoveries that incorporate many of the creativity principles identified above.

The innovation tunnel: a trip into the unknown

As the maker/faker parable at the opening of this chapter illustrated, innovation involves taking a journey into the unknown. You enter the innovation tunnel without quite knowing where you are going to come out. Just as with an act of artistic creation, there is no preordained finishing point.

While no one can say when or how the breakthrough idea will be sparked, enough is known about the situations and context when these kinds of events are likely to occur. Part of the special nature of the innovation tunnel is to simulate events that optimise the chances when these big ideas can occur. By basing the events on appropriate experiential events that move people through humour, conflict, collaborative problem-solving, relaxation and fun at different times in the programme, the group has an opportunity to get into the creative zone when inspiration occurs naturally.

For the same reasons that the brand dream process is staged at an inspiring location, the place where the innovation tunnel is staged is selected purposefully for its unusual or exceptional features. The event normally lasts one or two days. Typically, it involves all the team working on an innovation project – from brand managers and marketers to product development people inside the organisation plus representatives from any relevant partners outside the company.

Location, the place that you start the process and enter the tunnel, is all-important. Just as artists, writers and musicians choose to work in places that are inspiring and relaxing, so the best ideas are likely to be produced in settings that put people in the right frame of mind. Offices and factories are designed with efficiency and productivity in mind. If you are in an unfamiliar setting, everything looks different. It allows the creative team to put on different lenses and see things with new eyes.

They are not designed to be crucibles of innovation. Despite the fact that some managers may not understand the need to seek out locations away from the office, in the wrong place, especially the familiar working environment, innovation sessions turn out to be enervating and counter-productive.

There are other reasons why location is important. Creativity cannot be summoned to order. It is most likely to be stimulated when people are relaxed and not subjected to the usual pressures of working life. Besides, as the above examples of breakthroughs from the worlds of business, science and the arts show, ideas have a habit of appearing at the most unexpected times: relaxation rather than brainstorming can be more conducive to generating inspired insights.

As well as location, the innovation tunnel sets out to create conditions that stimulate people to make imaginative connections and come up with inspired ideas. Disruptive events – whether arguments, having to deal with an alcoholic landlord or being cut off by the snow in a ski chalet – unplanned or out-of-the-ordinary, can change the dynamics within a group with dramatic and beneficial consequences. Rather like Big Brother, tensions arise, people are thrown together, different relationships are forged, and we make sure that the creative process is the winner. Because the camaraderie is intensified as a result of the bonding that occurs, there is an intense desire to get the job done well.

We also use portals to connect product strategy and consumer insight. These metaphorical gateways are constructed around a theme that challenges the group to come up with unconventional thinking. For example with a toy maker, the group moved through a succession of portals to explore a range of propositions including the question, 'When is a toy not a toy?' Another was built round the theme, 'Be the boss'. The outcome from that was the recommendation to develop a product that was wholly owned by the company, rather than being licensed from other manufacturers, a feature of the company's practice up till then.

The following example shows how the innovation tunnel process has been used in practice. In this case, the goal was to give people the confidence to believe that they can be innovative, whatever their formal role in the organisation. This was the starting point for Natalie Bentley, Nestlé's beverage innovation manager responsible for coffee, hot chocolate and other beverages. Her aim was to change the whole way people in her marketing team thought about the creative process and their ability to be more innovative in their approach to work.

Getting into the spirit of innovation

Although Natalie was familiar with a number of methods and techniques for managing innovation, these mostly majored on the post-idea phase. 'Managing the process and learning how to get ideas through the business are all well and good. We had previously experienced different methods of innovation which involved set ways of delivering an idea. But they were often very restrictive.'

A preliminary discussion involving an exchange of experiences and thoughts on the mysteries of successful innovation confirmed Natalie in her opinion that she should try a completely different approach that provided people with an entirely fresh perspective on the creative process. 'As a business, we are not good at getting out of our comfort zone. It presents a risk for some people.' The result was the organisation of a 'spirit of innovation' day when the team of 25 marketing people were introduced to concepts and ideas that they could explore directly themselves.

Following a scene-setting discussion of the creative process, the day was structured around a number of experiential events. 'I had no advance knowledge of what we were going to be doing,' says Natalie.

One of the goals for the day was to show people what they could achieve with an open-ended project when they allowed their intuition to guide them to an outcome that was neither preordained nor imposed. Corporations thrive on direction, objectives and outcomes. Enabling the team to try out a situation where they allowed themselves to get into a freewheeling frame of mind was part of the programme for the event.

In one exercise, members of the group were given a number of materials and scissors and just asked to go and create something without any specific end point. 'Some people found it difficult to know what to do when they were not asked to produce something specific,' says Natalie. 'But others just got on with it.' Throughout the spirit of innovation day, the group were involved in a number of similar projects with touchy-feely goals. 'The whole idea was to take them out of their comfort zone, challenge and stimulate them to think more creatively.'

The experience affected people in different ways. 'Even our marketing director has quoted back to me that you can have a flexible goal and that it is not always necessary to fix on an end point. Some people understood why we were doing things this way, but felt they were not creative people.' For others, it was a liberating experience. 'It wasn't quite my goal, but some saw how this could help them in their private lives as well.'

Having given the team a taste of what open-ended innovation was like, the spirit of innovation day was followed up with something that tested both their ability to come up with ideas but also be passionate about them and sell them in a compelling way. For this phase of the programme, the setting was a version of the Dragon's Den. 'They had no prior notice. The requirement was to come up with a business idea and present it to a panel,' says Natalie. 'It was the same objective: to challenge them and get them thinking.'

Despite the reaction that they needed more time for preparation, the spontaneous nature of the event won out and the competitive momentum it produced swept people along. 'It turned out to be a really stimulating day with some great ideas. Some people have definitely taken what they learnt in these two days back into their office lives.'

The bottom-line result was that this highly interactive experiential programme opened people up to the emotional side of creativity and their personal capabilities. 'It definitely challenged a lot of old-fashioned thinking about innovation.'

In common with the brand dream process, experiential learning plays a major role in innovation tunnel projects. Finding out what real innovation is about is best discovered through getting involved in the act of creation, without a fixed goal or a preordained end point.

Innovation only comes alive when the output is translated into successful products in the marketplace. Our approach to obtaining input into the process from consumers involves a similar experience-based approach to discovering consumer insights.

Why consumer boot camps turn up better answers

But what does the consumer think? Without enthusiastic customers, there is no business. The question is what role the consumer should play in influencing the development of a brand or an innovative product. Weaker brands are constantly being led by the consumer. Strong brands tell the consumer what the brand is about: this is our dream.

There is all the difference between being confident about your brand dream and looking for input that will help you achieve your goals as opposed to checking whether it is right or wrong.

The consumer boot camp process was developed to help companies get the right kinds of answers to the brand and product questions. In common with the brand dream model and innovation tunnel, it is based on a collaborative and experiential approach. In this case, the aim is to involve the brand owner and the team with the consumer interactively. This is the real antidote to the stale focus group formula. Consumer boot camps put customers through their paces in ways that they find entertaining and fun for them, and genuinely insightful for the brand team.

For example, a conventional approach to finding out what people would like from a zoo visit would involve quizzing them on their views. You are likely to get fairly predictable and ultimately unhelpful answers from a focus group or interview set-up. But if you first gave them an opportunity to see *Jurassic Park* or fired their imagination in some other way, their responses are going to be more colourful and imaginative.

Giving consumers different, unusual perspectives on what you want them to express views about can be highly effective. In another project for a media company, two contrasting thought zones were created: one simulated a dark cave, the other an up-in-the-clouds hot air balloon. The idea was that these different physical locations prompted different mind-sets and provided contrasting perspectives on people's reactions to new service ideas.

In the case of a consumer product company, the event pivoted around story telling to help consumers communicate their reactions in a fun, deeper, more powerful way with the facilitator. The boot camp approach gets much deeper into the consumer psyche than sitting around with a cup of tea and a biscuit.

The point about both the innovation tunnel and consumer boot camps is that they move people beyond the familiar and everyday into a space where they can allow their imaginations full play. From any organisation's point of view, faking is only ever going to take them so far. Finally, they will run out of road with incremental improvements and enhancements. By then, unless they have learnt how to make innovation part of their culture, it could just be too late to discover the magic of inspirational creativity.

RENEWING THE DREAM

At some point, every dream has to end. What you don't want to happen is for the curtain to come down prematurely, or until all the opportunities have been realised. As we have repeatedly stressed throughout this book, it is essential to nurture and sustain your brand dream with care and attention. But from time to time it will need to be renewed, refocused and repaired to keep it running. So you have taken the brand dream medicine and it worked. However, that was a time ago and now the business environment is different. There are several reasons for revisiting the brand dream.

Changes in corporate circumstances, perhaps a merger or an acquisition, could trigger the need to go back to first principles. Or a major upheaval in the marketplace may make a second look essential. It could be the impact of a disruptive technology. The brand may simply be running out of steam after a long-running period of success. At some point, for one or more of these reasons, your brand dream may start to look vulnerable. The solution is to revisit the model and ask what changes in the business factors alter the make-up and balance of the three brand dream components.

When you've got a Richard Branson or Steve Jobs on board, they know instinctively when it is time to look afresh at the brand, take in new directions or build on established success. More than that, the evangelism flows constantly from the top so that the dream is constantly communicated. But for companies without that brand evangelist driving the enterprise, it can be a challenge.

So how do you know in other circumstances when the time has come to renew the brand dream?

There will come a point which is apparent to any senior manager, when a brand is in trouble or underperforming because sales are slumping and customers are defecting. Waiting till the eleventh hour to take action is always risky. There is always a temptation to look outside for answers. But all the market research in the world will not bail you out unless you know why your brand is underperforming from a position of deep knowledge of its strengths and weaknesses.

In these circumstances, the job of renewal will be much easier if members of the core team who developed the original model are still working in the organisation. But the odds are that some, perhaps all, will have moved on. They are the people who know the issues and assumptions underlying the model intimately. When those key people have left, along with them goes the knowledge and experience that went into building the brand dream model, the underlying assumptions and key insights.

It is rather like watching the sandcastle you have built on the beach being washed away by the incoming tide. Of course, there will still be the representation of the brand dream, traditions and behaviour on paper. But what really counts is the internalisation of the significance of those words. The brand dream is a living organic entity.

Companies can take measures to safeguard the brand dream and preserve that tradition of knowledge and understanding.

For example, ensuring that there is always a succession of brand guardians and evangelists in the company who can pass the baton on in the event of their departure is one important measure. Anyone who is passionate about the brand and who understands the genius of the brand, not necessarily the brand manager but someone on whom the original brand dream process had made a major impact, can take on this role.

Another insurance against this absolute loss of knowledge is by enrolling as many people within the organisation in the brand dream as possible. For one thing there is no point in creating an exclusive club, a kind of brand dream business class that leaves the rest of the organisation feeling they are missing out. Everyone who touches the brand – from marketing, customer service to despatch and outside agencies – needs to know what the brand is about.

So there will come a time when the only way to re-energise the company is by rerunning the brand dream programme with a new team and a new generation of employees.

The message is simple. If you want to keep succeeding, never stop dreaming.

INDEX

Index